Blessed Are the Chickenhearted

and 99 Other Beatitudes for Everyday Living

BETTY POWELL

Kregel
PUBLICATIONS

Grand Rapids, MI 49501

Blessed Are the Chickenhearted and 99 Other Beatitudes for Everyday Living

Copyright © 1999 by Betty Powell

Published by Kregel Publications, a division of Kregel, Inc., P.O. Box 2607, Grand Rapids, MI 49501. Kregel Publications provides trusted, biblical publications for Christian growth and service. Your comments and suggestions are valued.

For more information about Kregel Publications, visit our web site at www.kregel.com

Cover and book design: Frank Gutbrod

Library of Congress Cataloging-in-Publication Data
Powell, Betty M.
    Blessed are the chickenhearted and 99 other beatitudes for everyday living / by Betty Powell.
        p.   cm.
        1. Christian life.   I. Title.
BV4501.2.P5598   1999   242—dc 21   98-50465
                                                                        CIP

ISBN 0-8254-3553-6

Printed in the United States of America

1 2 3 4 5 / 03 02 01 00 99

Contents

Contents

Preface

I am profoundly grateful to the Lord for all the privileges enjoyed in my lifetime. With my late husband, Dr. Ivor Powell, who was known internationally as "the man from Wales," I was able to visit many countries preaching the glorious gospel of the grace of God. What I learned has been reproduced in this volume. I have always kept scrapbooks in which I write everything of outstanding importance. My husband's office was destroyed by fire several years ago, but most of its contents were miraculously preserved; although charred and damaged, my writings were usable. God surely had a purpose in protecting those notebooks.

Most of my readers will not have had the privilege of traveling extensively in other parts of the world, so I will try to escort them, in thought, to the places that I have seen. Perhaps along the journey, they will hear the voice of the Son of God speaking through these beatitudes.

My husband and I visited the stately cathedrals of Europe as well as the mystical land of India where extreme wealth and abject poverty exist side by side. We worked for three years in Australia, two in New Zealand, and four in Africa. It

7

was our privilege to be the official evangelists of the Baptist churches in those countries, and in that capacity we saw so much of importance. It was a joy and a blessing to visit missionaries on their stations, to lead crusades in major cities, and to witness miracles that only the grace of God could perform.

It was an emotional and thrilling experience to visit the land of Israel and to be in the places where the Savior ministered so long ago. We saw the amazing pyramids in Egypt and viewed the national treasures in the famous museum in Cairo. It is my fervent wish that all my readers will capture the charm and excitement of those unforgettable experiences.

I have always enjoyed writing about the Savior. Most of these beatitudes first appeared in the monthly magazine formerly produced by our crusades. Over the years many friends have requested that these messages be preserved in a more permanent form, but my husband and I were so busy traveling and conducting evangelistic meetings that little attention was given to the appeals. Yet, undeterred, people from near and far have repeated their desires, and it is no longer possible to ignore their requests. Compiling this volume has revived memories of yesteryear and has enabled me to live again those experiences. May great blessing follow this publication, enriching others who are serving the Master.

I also want to thank the president of Kregel Publications in Grand Rapids, Michigan, Mr. James Kregel, and his lovely wife, Kathie, who are among my choicest friends.

Betty Powell
Santa Barbara, California

Blessed Are They Who Have a Friend

She was just a young teenage girl, but she was beautiful. It was her bewitching, compelling serenity that first attracted my attention as I stood waiting at the store counter. She wore a loose-fitting blouse and jeans; her hair was tied up in little curlers, and she was looking straight ahead. Had she been able to see those curlers, I know she would have done a much better job—but she was blind! All the time I watched her, she never uttered a sound. Upright, dignified, contented, there she stood with her right hand lightly resting on the arm of the boy who was waiting for his hamburger and french fries. Suddenly—I think he was her brother—the boy said, "Want one?" She silently shook her head, and the little smile that followed was like a ray of sunlight shining across a darkened sky at dawn. Soon the hamburger was delivered, and the boy and girl walked away. All the while her hand never left his arm. She was quite content; she trusted him implicitly. The lad seemed a bit gruff, but if danger had threatened I think he would have given his life for that young lady. She trusted him, and he knew it. She had a friend.

Mary Ann Evans, who wrote under the name George Eliot (1819–1880), wrote a marvelous verse about friendship. She said:

FRIENDSHIP
Is the comfort, the inexpressible comfort
    of feeling safe with a person.
Having neither to weigh thoughts nor
    measure words,
But pouring all right out just as they are,
Chaff and grain together, certain that a faithful,
    friendly hand will take and sift them,
Keep what is worth keeping, and with a breath
    of comfort, blow the rest away.

Jehoram, king of Judah, ascended the throne when he was thirty-two years old; he reigned eight years, and "he died without being desired" (2 Chron. 21:20). He had no friends. What a lonely man he must have been. It has been well said that they who live to themselves will one day be left to themselves. Blessed indeed is the person who has real friends; trustworthy, loyal, dependable friends are a treasure of great worth. When you read these simple words, start counting. How many real friends do you possess? It is written that Moses had a Friend. That Friend was God. You may be as the blind girl; you may not be able to see far ahead—but keep your hand on his arm. He will lead you aright.

Blessed Are They Who Live One Day at a Time

I hardly know where the old year went, but it has surely gone somewhere! All through my Christian life I have approached each new year with a certain amount of questioning. I suppose it is natural to look ahead and wonder what will take place before the end of December. Sometimes it seemed as if I had to climb a great mountain, endure a terrible storm, or carry a burden that weighed tons. The very idea was oppressing, and perhaps you are feeling like that even now.

Many years ago, a Swedish author fantasized about an investigation made by the face of a clock. The timepiece had ceased to work, and the face of the clock was determined to find out why. He discovered that the pendulum had ceased swinging. Since he had to swing back and forth every second, he would have to do this eighty-six thousand times a day. The thought had overwhelmed him, so he stopped.

The face of the clock then asked the pendulum to swing just five times, and he did so. "Was that hard on you?" asked the face. "No," replied the pendulum. "But what wears me down is the thought of making eighty-six thousand a day, and two and a half million a month." Then the face said, "But you do not have to make more than one swing at a time, and you have the strength to do that. So do it, and face the difficulties of the future only as they come." Then the pendulum went to work again, realizing that he had been foolish. He could make one swing at a time and that was all that was necessary. "Be not anxious for the morrow" said the Lord. "As thy days, so shall thy strength be." Live one day at a time!

> Dream not too much of what you'll do tomorrow,
> How well perhaps you'll do another year.
> Tomorrow's chance you do not need to borrow;
> Today is here.
> Boast not too much of mountains you will master
> The time you linger in this world below:
> To dream is well, but doing brings us faster
> To where we go.
> Swear not some day to break some habit fetter
> When this old year is dead and passed away.
> But if you really want to live much better,
> Begin today.

I have often heard it said that God never gives December grace in June; he never supplies mountain strength when one is traveling through the prairies. When we reach the mountains God *then* will give us added strength to climb; when we reach the storms, he will give us endurance. As thy days—so shall thy strength be. Let us believe this and live with this assurance. Then it really will be a happy new year.

Blessed Are They Whose Snow Is White

"Mother, mother, the snow is sick!" The small boy who uttered the strange and frightening cry could not have known his words were destined to arouse a nation. After World War II, the little land of Norway, which for years had been occupied by the Nazis, faced a monumental task. When the enemy was driven out, the Norwegians were left with a shattered economy and a very bleak future. Something drastic had to be done quickly! New factories, new industries began making their appearance throughout the country, and slowly the nation began to recover. Yet, in those early postwar years, few, if any, of the politicians even considered the price to be paid for the new prosperity. As far as they were concerned, the ecology was nonexistent. Waste dumped into the fjords killed the fish; poisonous fumes released into the atmosphere went unnoticed—and then came the *gray snow*. It was catastrophic and it disturbed a complacent nation. Very strong winds had brought pollution from the factories of Germany to darken the snows of southern Norway. It took years for the nation to recover.

As our tour leader explained all this during a journey we took from Bergen to Oslo, it was easy to visualize that awful pollution spoiling the beautiful land of Norway. But then, as I considered the matter, I wondered how often this type of thing takes place in our own private world. Nasty gossip, unfriendly criticism, backbiting, slander, and other clouds of pollution can escape in an unwise moment, and although we may never know the effects, Satan's winds will carry that pollution to darken and spoil lives far away. I often wonder how many growing children are lost to Christ and the church because of the smog released at the Sunday lunch table! Many parents often wonder why their married children never attend church. Could it be that their polluted conversation, carried by evil winds, colored the thoughts of their own offspring? Blessed is the person whose snow is white.

The same kind of thing happened in New Zealand during our stay in the southern hemisphere. The people of that beautiful land will never forget the day when *red rain* discolored the green fields of the countryside. It was unbelievable and yet true. Thousands of miles away, in the heart of Australia's desert, hurricane-force winds had whipped the red sand into the upper atmosphere where strong currents of air drove the "pollution" to faraway New Zealand. Nothing could be done about that particular catastrophe, but fortunately something was done about the German chimneys.

There are some disappointing things in life we cannot change, but other things can be prevented. Surely it is the duty of every one of us to do what is possible to keep the snow white.

Blessed Are They Who Know Where They Are Going

When I attended school in Barry, Wales, I often read of the ancient Vikings who terrorized the inhabitants of Britain. Those strange, wild men of the sea would land on our eastern shores to pillage and steal all they could find. The early Britons hated them. Little did I know then that one day I would actually see some of the ships that carried these Norse invaders. Just a few years ago, I went with my husband to the amazing Viking Museum at Bygdoy, Oslo, Norway, and I shall never forget what I saw there.

The author Anders Hagen, in his book *The Viking Ship Finds*, wrote:

> Of all the thousands of ships that sailed along the Northern coasts in Viking times (800–1000 A.D.)—only three have been preserved. All three had been drawn ashore and used as burial ships for well-to-do people. They had been buried with the dead and covered with large

15

quantities of stones, clay and turf. This is the
reason why the ships have been preserved so
well. The most famous of the three Viking craft
is known as "The Oseberg Ship." It is thought
that this was the burial place of the Viking
Queen Aasa and alas, of her servant who was
buried alive! Christianity had not reached the
Nordic lands in those early times, but from the
artifacts discovered in the Queen's ship, it is
perfectly clear the Vikings believed death was
the start of a long journey. They did not know
where their queen was going, but she was going somewhere! Therefore, they buried with
her "spades, a refuse sled, and all kinds of uten-
sils from the kitchen. Dishes, dippers, buckets,
cauldrons, a frying pan, knives, and many other
items." In the burial chamber lay beds, pillows,
quilts, and clothes. There were strips of tapes-
try, knitting needles, and all kinds of things to
prevent boredom on the long journey to somewhere! There were two lamps (iron) mounted
on long rods, a small, wooden wool holder, a
large comb, a big pair of iron scissors, a yarn
winder and several looms. There were three
beautiful sleighs, a working sled and a heavy
cart. Fifteen horses, four dogs, and an ox had
been driven in from pasture, their throats had
been cut, and the bodies buried with the Queen.
She would need them wherever she was going.

Now, after all these centuries, these things have been uncovered by the archaeologists and are being studied in the Viking
Ship Hall at Bygdoy. The Norwegian people now realize Queen
Aasa never used the lavish collection of articles provided by
her devoted subjects. But they still believe she went *somewhere*
without them. Long ago, Job asked the question: "If a man die,
shall he live again?" Even today, millions of people speculate

regarding a life beyond the grave. They ask: "Is there such a life? Is there such a place? If so, how do we get there? What must we do?" Blessed is the one who knows.

Paul said that while "we are at home in the body, we are absent from the Lord." He predicted our mortal bodies eventually would be clothed with immortality and death would be swallowed up in victory. Thank God, I shall not need my fry pan in heaven! I shall sit at his table and feed on the Bread of Life.

Blessed Are They Who Forgive Their Enemies

Reverend Wurmbrand, who was imprisoned for fourteen years in Rumania, has written the following story:

> We were thirty Christians in a small prison cell—one day the door opened and a new prisoner was pushed in.
>
> It took us a little while to recognize him in the semidarkness of the cell. When we did, we were amazed to see the captain of the secret police who had arrested and tortured many of us. We asked him what had happened; how he came to be here, a prisoner like ourselves.
>
> He said that one day a twelve-year-old boy had asked permission to see him. He carried a pot of flowers and was very shy. Eventually, he said, "Comrade Captain, you are the one who arrested my father and mother, and today is my mother's birthday. It has always been my

habit to buy her a pot of flowers on her birthday, but now, because of you, I have no mother to make happy—so I thought these flowers might make the mother of your children happy. Please take them to your wife."

I was stunned, and the lad, seeing my perplexity said, "My mother was a Christian and she taught me that we must love our enemies and reward evil with good." The captain took the boy's flowers, and with tears in his eyes, embraced him. Truth and love will vibrate, even in a Communist's heart. The process of remorse and conversion had begun. He could no longer arrest innocent men; he could no longer inflict torture on Christians. Finally, he had arrived in prison with us because he, the atheist torturer, had become the defender of Christians.

It would seem that neither an aggressive gospel nor a new theology will carry Christianity into the new century; only the actual living-out of Christ's new commandment will do that. He said, "Love your enemies and do good to those who hate you."

Ahead of us is a new year and many people will be making resolutions. Some will be good, others may not be; some will be kept, others quickly forgotten. The story of the little boy's pot of flowers was quoted at a conference at which my husband was speaking in Largs, Scotland, and as I considered its implications, a desire arose within my heart to love everybody. Actually, I do not think I have enemies, but if anybody displeases me, I hope I shall love them as God does—with an everlasting love.

Sin has a great many tools, but an unforgiving spirit is the handle that fits them all.

Blessed Are They Who Abide

E rosion is a serious danger no matter where it is found. Its working sometimes can be so subtle and so well concealed that when eventually it strikes, the results can be devastating. Termites, dry rot, burrowing creatures, and such go quietly about their business, but the end is always the same. In a recent evening paper, I saw a small paragraph concerning the mighty Matterhorn. It said, "The Matterhorn in the Swiss-Italian Alps is self-destructing. As avalanches wear away its softer lower slopes, the mountain's upper pyramid acquires more of an overhang. Someday, the massive 'horn' may topple."

What a shame that this object of awe-inspiring grandeur, this mountain which has attracted innumerable climbers, this evidence of God's unsurpassed handiwork, should one day fall. If I may move from the sublime to the almost ridiculous, I am reminded of my own garden. I had worked very hard making it into a thing of beauty only to discover one morning that a gopher had come up during the night to ruin my beautiful lawn.

When I first went to Queensland, Australia, I wondered why all the houses were on stilts. My inexperience suggested that height might be extremely dangerous in a wind storm. I was quickly assured it would be even more dangerous if the house stood on the ground. The deadly termites in Australia have a particular liking for the foundations of wooden structures. The elevation of the home enables the owner to walk beneath the floors on regular inspection tours.

It seems a shame that some householders should be more concerned about their temporary dwelling than they are with their spiritual temple.

David, that very attractive and lovely shepherd boy, grew to be a greatly admired king, yet one day he self-destructed because he had neglected to search for termites in the foundations of his soul. A little self-examination is good for all of us. If we become aware of the dangers within, there is some chance that the dry rot, the termites, the enemies, might be destroyed before they destroy us.

The Bible is filled with stories of this kind. King Saul, chosen to be Israel's first monarch, continued to slide until the downward momentum carried him beyond the limits of recovery. Poor Judas—he became so intent on lifting the offering, so to speak, he forgot to kneel at the altar. Yet no person can be self-righteous, for the Bible warns us to take care that no one steals our crown. "Let him that thinketh he standeth take heed lest he fall" (1 Cor. 10:12). Blessed indeed is the one who abides— not here today and gone tomorrow, but always reliable, continuing, trustworthy, and a joy to the heart of God.

Blessed Are They Who Walk a Country Mile

Recently as I listened to a commercial on television, my mind began thinking about a new beatitude. A lady was testing a certain product and was obviously pleased. "It beats the other brand by a country mile," she boasted. Probably most of the viewers did not even notice the details which impressed me, for the term "a country mile" has become commonplace in our language. Nevertheless, for people who have traveled in other lands, this saying is most eloquent.

As I listened to the speaker, I thought of Africa where my husband and I often journeyed for days in order to reach the cities where our crusades were to be held. Often we became very weary on those dusty roads, and whenever it was possible we asked a passer-by where we could find a restaurant—hotel—cafe—any place where we could rest and eat. I shall always remember one helpful person who said, "Just go round the next corner and you will be there in no time." The next corner was twenty-four miles from the restaurant. In a vast land, distances to one born there are almost meaningless. "Just up the road" could mean an hour's journey, and "around the corner" could mean anything. A country mile does not necessarily mean "a mile in the country;" it could mean a day's journey. As I thought about this, I wondered how long it had been since I went a country mile to help someone. The Lord tells us in Matthew 5:41: "And whosoever shall compel thee to go a mile, go with him twain [two]." In actual experience, I wonder how far that would be. The Savior also provided a glowing example of "a country mile" when he spoke of the Good Samaritan. This illustrious Bible character not only saw a man in urgent and desperate need—he went to him, he bound up his wounds, he poured in oil and wine, he set him upon his own beast, he brought him to an inn, took care of him, paid the bill, and accepted responsibility for any future liability, saying, "Take care of him, and whatsoever thou spendest more, when I come again, I will repay thee" (Luke 10:34–35). The Bible does not say how many miles of travel were involved in this rescue operation. Probably only the Lord himself could assess the length of that happy and thrilling road of service.

Then, suddenly, I thought of another who went many country miles to rescue us. His journey brought him from the ivory palaces, and took him to a green hill—and he never gave up. The Lord Jesus really knew the joy of service. It is recorded of him: "Who for the joy that was set before him endured the cross" (Heb. 12:2).

If you get the chance to go a country mile today—look for company on the road.

Blessed Are They Who Forgive

Egeskov Castle, thirty miles outside of the city of Odense in Denmark, is a most picturesque, though forbidding place. Its tall turrets silhouetted against a blue sky, the moat that completely surrounds the thick, stone walls, and the magnificent gardens throughout the area present the visitor with one of the greatest tourist attractions in Denmark. I shall never forget the day when I stood alongside the castle, gazing at a very small window high up in the wall. I shuddered when I thought of the awful tragedy that had taken place in the tiny room behind that window. The original builder was said to be a Dutchman named Martin Bussart, but the castle ultimately became the home of Frands Brockenhuus, the governor of the province. His son, Laureds, who inherited the place after his father's death, was educated at a university and ultimately became the chancellor there. He had the reputation of being enormously strong, pious, and quick-tempered. His daughter, Rigborg, unfortunately drew his undying anger, and her pathetic situation attracts the sympathy of every woman. She had been seduced by Frederick Rosenkrantz of Rosenvold and gave birth to his child. When this became known, the king of Denmark—a friend of Frederick's—became infuriated, and ordered Rigborg's guardian to imprison her for life.

She was placed in her room and the door was walled in. A small opening was left so that her food could be pushed through to her. She stayed in that prison from the year 1599 until her father died in 1604. After his death, Rigborg's mother released her. Four years later she was permitted to attend a church service. She died in 1641. Today, that very small window high in the castle wall bears mute testimony to the harsh, brutal punishments of an earlier age. Mercy was almost unknown when law sat upon the throne.

The Bible tells of a similar incident. Jehoiachin, the king of Judah, was imprisoned for thirty-seven years, and there was no hope of his release until a monstrous king died. But "it came to pass . . . that Evil-merodach king of Babylon in the year that he began to reign did lift up the head of Jehoiachin king of Judah out of prison" (2 Kings 25:27–30). Forgiveness is one of the gentlest words in our language. Bitterness, grudges, revenge, and malice can tear the soul apart. They can blot out the sun and make the night eternal. Blessed indeed is the woman who keeps her spirit free; who resolutely refuses to hurt anyone.

Our Lord said: "Blessed are the merciful: for they shall obtain mercy" (Matt. 5:7). Actually, when we entertain unforgiving ideas, those ideas become prison bars around our own souls. We suffer more than the objects of our wrath. Blessed indeed are they who forgive.

> Words are things of little cost,
> Quickly spoken, quickly lost;
> We forget them, but they stand
> As witnesses at God's right hand.

Blessed Are They Who Remember

During our travels around the world, my husband and I saw many wonderful churches, but few, if any, surpassed the amazing cathedral at Uppsala, Sweden.

The elegant sanctuary was begun in A.D. 1270 and completed over 159 years later, in the year 1425. In 1702, a terrible fire destroyed most of the buildings in Uppsala, and the cathedral was severely damaged. The restoration of the edifice was effected in two stages. The architect in charge of the second phase, possibly wishing to improve on the ancient design, had added adornments of his own, but in the year 1970, these outside additions began to separate from the main building. Stones actually fell among people walking in the street. Obviously, something had to be done, and in 1974, the monumental task of cleaning and restoring the grand old church began. The experts soon discovered that the only safe way to cleanse the very dirty stone was by using fresh bread. A liquid might damage the ancient and often delicate stonework, but apparently the soft bread, straight from the ovens, performed miracles. The once very filthy masonry now gleams with a brightness that is unbelievable.

Perhaps the most moving sight of all is in the Donas chapel, adjoining the main church. High up the cleansed wall, the architect has deliberately left one dirty, rectangular stone. At first glance, it seems a big, black stain in an entrancingly beautiful church, but it is much more than that. When the work of restoration is finally finished and the church is presented in all its beauty to the authorities, that one, dirty stone is to remind the people of what used to be. The architect thought that without it, they might forget. When our guide related this fact, my soul was suddenly thrilled. I thought of another church, made of living—but alas, so often—soiled stones. Some day, as Paul said, Christ will "present it . . . a glorious church, not having spot, or wrinkle, or any such thing; but that it should be holy and without blemish" (Eph. 5:27). The work of cleansing and restoration will have been completed. How wonderful it is that the Divine Architect, who undertook the entire task of redemption, also desired us to remember forever what we once were and the price paid to finish the cleansing process. Not in us, but in him will be the everlasting reminder. We shall know by the print of the nails in his hands.

There will be neither crippled nor blind person there; no blemish will be in his finished work. Yet, when we look upon him whom our sins pierced, we shall remember the price he paid, and together exclaim: "Thou art worthy . . . for thou wast slain and hast redeemed us to God by thy blood, out of every kindred, and tongue, and people, and nation" (Rev. 5:9).

Blessed are they who remember this now. Blessed even more will be those who remember it for all eternity.

Blessed Are They Who Can Keep a Secret

True friends are among the choicest of earth's citizens, and happy indeed are they who are rich in this area. There are many distinguishing characteristics about such people, but perhaps the greatest of all is the trustworthiness that preserves secrets. It is always a temptation for souls of lesser worth to betray a confidence, or to violate a trust, especially when the secret involves some important detail of a person's private life. There are occasions when it is better to keep one's own secret; when none but God shares the thoughts of the human soul. Sometimes a cat out of the bag can do much damage.

Possibly, one of the best kept secrets of all time comes from Norway, where long ago the royal line of the Bernadette family lifted that picturesque land to heights of greatness hitherto unknown.

Marshal Jean-Baptiste Bernadette became Karl XIV, Johan, King of Sweden and Norway in 1818, and ruled for twenty-six years. He was greatly beloved and his wise leadership brought much happiness to his subjects. Throughout all the years, the monarch was exceedingly careful in preserving his greatest secret. He never swam in the ocean; he never bathed in public, and somehow he eluded medical examinations. Not until he died and the mortician began preparing the body for burial, were the tattoo marks on his chest discovered. As a young officer in the army, Jean-Baptiste was so infuriated with events taking place in the highest circles of society, that he had tattooed on his chest the words, *mort aux roix—death to kings*. At that stage of his life, the young man could never have guessed what he was to become. Nevertheless, when he ascended the throne, he determined as king to right all the wrongs of the court, and history testifies to the success of his efforts. But no one ever knew of the message on his chest. This was his secret. The words, *mort aux roix*, were never discovered until the monarch was gone.

There are many people whose past might arise to hinder and spoil life. The old saying: "Let sleeping dogs lie" is most eloquent. It is so reassuring to remember that tattoo marks are not left in God's record. He has promised that our sins will never again be remembered (see Jer. 31:34). The only record preserved in the presence of heaven's King is the marks of the nails in his hands. Thank God, our secrets have not been preserved; they have been blotted out.

Mother's Altar

Many years ago I knelt and bowed my head in
    prayer
Upon a checkered apron as my mother stroked
    my hair.
I have knelt at many altars of wood, of gold, of
    stone;
But that gingham-covered altar is the sweetest I
    have known.

Blessed Are They Who Cause Ripples

Have you ever thrown a pebble into the placid waters of a pool and watched as the ripples chase each other toward the distant banks? There is nothing more restful in the midst of a long and tiring walk than to sit in the shade of a tree on some grassy slope and throw stones into the water. To pick a daisy and pluck its petals; to watch a rabbit darting in and out of a bush; to listen to a bird or watch a fish jumping for a fly—all these things make crowded cities seem unattractive. Let me be honest and admit that I love to throw pebbles into a pool; I am always fascinated as I see the ever-widening ripples momentarily spoiling the reflections in the watery mirror. When the pool is large, I always wonder where the ripples will end—just how far will they go?

Recently, we received a booklet from New Zealand that told the amazing story of a marvelous youth camp. It exists because a dedicated Christian surrendered part of his farm to Christ, and by so doing, caused a ripple on a pond. When that land became available, other Christians were stirred, rolled up their sleeves, and began to work. Children who once attended that camp are now Christian workers in many parts of the world. Who can tell where the ripples on a pond will end?

Do you remember the ripple that Mary made when she brought a box of ointment to Christ? She was criticized and misunderstood, but the Lord recognized the love shining through her action. He knew that the ripples made that day would never end—they would reach out to the shores of all nations. He said, "Verily, I say unto you, wheresoever this gospel shall be preached in the whole world, there shall also this, that this woman hath done, be told for a memorial of her" (Matt. 26:13). Mary had no idea of the far-reaching effects of her action, and probably the men gathered there would have scoffed at any suggestion of the greatness of her act. She had thrown a small pebble of devotion into a worldwide pool. As the Lord considered her deed, he might have asked where the ripples would end on that pond—but he didn't, because he knew they would never end.

Some people think they are not very successful in their endeavors for Christ. We must never jump to hasty conclusions. Many have been laughed at for Christ's sake; some have suffered and others have lost family and friends, but none of this has happened in vain. Even if we cannot see all the outgoing ripples, God can. He traces the path of every one. Perhaps we shall be thrilled some day when the Lord begins to unfold the mysteries of his unending grace. A gift in America might have led to a soul in India. A word spoken might have left an impression on a man's soul—an impression destined to deepen until he became a Christian. Who can tell where and when the ripples on a pond will end?

Blessed Are They Who Share

The Bible says, "Bear ye one another's burdens, and so fulfill the law of Christ" (Gal. 6:2). During the last week, this thought has come to me in a very forceful way. In the midst of a world that is filled with sick and weary people, our sympathetic understanding is often very superficial. We think: *What a shame;* we offer a quick little prayer, and within moments have proceeded on our merry little way. I have heard Christians saying: "I am bored; I haven't anything to do." My immediate reaction is one of envy—I say: "I wish I were like that." But suddenly I become ashamed that such a thought ever entered my mind. There is no reason whatsoever why every Christian cannot be a full-time worker for Christ. In one way or another all can work for the Savior. I read some time ago about a little girl whose small playmate from the neighbor's house had died. When her mother asked where she had been, the tiny tot replied: "I've been in to see Elsie's Mamma." Amazed, the mother asked: "What did you say to her?" "Nothing, I just climbed up into her lap and cried with her." Probably that little girl's tears were more eloquent than the pastor's sermon.

We are surrounded by people who need words of comfort, cheer, and encouragement. Sometimes just a handshake or a get-well card through the mail can help people realize they are not alone with their problems. Somehow, I cannot escape the thought that when we are truly tuned in to heaven, when we are really God's instruments, each and every day we can be a part of a miracle. Surely, to be used by God is the greatest privilege that can ever come our way.

During the years of World War II, my husband and I were in charge of a church in Wales. We became aware of the need of another minister whose church was twenty-seven miles away in one of the coal-mining valleys of the area. The stress and strain of life had caused a severe nervous breakdown, and that pastor's outlook seemed rather bleak. He had no money to finance a vacation, yet his physical condition demanded that a rest be forthcoming. Well, we invited him to come to our seaside home, and naturally he was thrilled to accept. I was more than willing to help him, but nevertheless I was very worried because at that time our food was severely rationed. If I were to strengthen that ailing minister, I needed special supplies and obviously I had no way of obtaining these. I could only pray and trust the Lord to help me.

The day before our guest was due to arrive, I heard a knock on our door, and when I answered, there stood one of our church members. Very timidly, she held out a shopping basket and said, "I hope you don't mind, but this is something I just have to do. The Lord has been telling me for two weeks that I should share some of my abundance with you. As you know I have several small children who do not have large appetites, and for weeks I have seen my food reserves increasing. I have lots of canned milk, butter, and eggs, and I knew I would not have peace of mind unless I shared this surplus with you. Please accept it as from the Lord."

When I explained to her the reality of my great need, we sat together and shed tears of joy. The Lord surely used this friend to perform what, to me, was a very important miracle. That woman and I had been sisters in the Lord before, but after that incident, there was a much closer bond between us—we were comrades in arms.

Is there someone in your world looking for you? Has the Master been waiting for the chance to use your feet, your hands, your tongue, to answer someone's prayer?

Blessed Are They Who Never Kill a Friend

Peter, an adventuresome young American, had a great ambition—to visit and climb the Swiss Alps. He worked hard and saved money to make his dreams come true, and eventually, the greatest day of his life dawned. When he arrived at his hotel, he was overwhelmed by the wall of whiteness that towered above him, reaching apparently to the blue sky. He could hardly believe his good fortune. He was there at last. Unfortunately, he was so filled with self-confidence and delight, that one day he ventured out alone and was caught in a blizzard. Wearily, he trudged on, knowing that if he stopped he might perish in the storm. Unable to find shelter of any kind, he walked until his last ounce of energy was gone, and then, utterly exhausted, he collapsed. As the snow began to cover his body, he knew he was in great danger, but suddenly he became aware of something nudging and licking his face. His drowsiness gave way to fear, and he opened his eyes to look into other eyes glaring down at him. Alas, he panicked—was this a wolf? Was it a bear? He grabbed his hunting knife and, with every bit of his remaining energy, struck at the animal's heart. The dog—for dog it was—

groaned and rolled over beside the frightened young man. Peter struggled to sit up, and then gasped as he saw, lying beside him, one of the rescue dogs used by the hospice at the great St. Bernard Pass. Its massive head now lay still in the snow; its thick coat was stained with blood, and there around its neck, was the little barrel of nourishing food carried by all the dogs in the rescue squads from the famous monastery.

Sobbing, Peter said, "I have killed a friend. I have killed a friend."

During the recent Holy Week, as we all prepared to remember the death and resurrection of our Lord, I found this story and it stirred my soul. I thought of the One who came down from the warmth of his heavenly home to rescue people who were lost and dying in the storms of life. His love brought him to the side of helpless people, but they killed him. He would have nourished and saved their souls; he would have restored them to health and happiness, but they nailed him to a cross. He wanted to help, but they crucified him.

Sometimes we are tempted to accuse the people who crucified Christ, but can we really do this when today we may be guilty of the same crime? Life is filled with choices. We are constantly faced with moments of decision, moments when we have to choose between Christ and our Barabbas. If only we would pause to think before we hastily act. There are occasions when our unwise, hasty actions hurt our best Friend— when we crucify all over again our dearest and best Helper. When we do that, we turn our back on the only chance we have of regaining the health and the happiness we have lost.

And perhaps there is another lesson we can learn from Peter's unfortunate experience. We should never walk alone when we are traveling in the hills and valleys of life. Let the Lord himself be our guide. Let him go before—*it's the only way to travel.*

Blessed Are They Who Know

Our Yuletide feast was over, but a tired little mother was resolutely determined to be in charge of the mopping-up operation. She had had a busy day. Rising early to get a good start with her preparations she soon discovered that her oven had gone wrong. It had taken over an hour to rectify matters, but then, with loving hands, she proceeded to make the most wonderful Christmas dinner. She secretly watched as we all enjoyed her meal, and her sparkling eyes evidenced her great happiness.

Now a mountainous stack of dirty dishes, pots and pans, and all the paraphernalia of cooking awaited attention. We tried to coax her to rest, but she continued to roll up her sleeves. Her son, Paul, whispered, "Leave her alone; she wants to do it." She stood in front of the kitchen sink like an army general about to slay a battalion of enemies. She was supremely happy; this was nothing new; she had lived her long life making sure that everyone of her family had enough to eat. As I watched her, it was so easy to love that wonderful mother.

My husband quoted a text from the gospel of Matthew: "Inasmuch as ye have done it unto one of the least of these my brethren, ye have done it unto me. . . . I was an hungered, and ye gave me meat" (Matt. 25:40, 35). He asked her son to translate this into Hungarian so that the mother would understand. "Tell her" he said "she has just cooked a dinner for the Lord."

Paul did as he was requested and his mother looked at us, smiled radiantly and said, "I know." Her statement was far more eloquent than a sermon. *She knew.* When she placed her hands into the dishwater, she was placing a crown upon the head of her Lord.

Many people will have accepted so much this Christmas without realizing the great amount of love behind the gift. The Marthas will have been up and doing whilst others have merely sat around talking.

Lenna Rees has written some great words:

> Let me grow lovely, growing old;
> So many fine things to do;
> Ivory, gold, and lace, and silk,
> They're better not being new.
> Beautiful too, are full-grown trees;
> Old streets a glamour hold.
> So why can't I as well as they
> Be lovely growing old?

Blessed indeed is the one who knows: how to grow old gracefully; how to talk with the Lord when sleep is evasive; how to see privilege in pain and delight in drudgery; how to see Christ when other people are convinced of his absence. Blessed is the one who knows how to grasp an invisible hand; how to smile into an invisible face. Blessed is the one who knows how to listen to infinite whispers; who knows and believes that each year will be another opportunity to serve the King of Kings.

Blessed Are They Who Are Remembered

Through the many years I accompanied my husband around the world, I systematically gathered anecdotes and other materials for a scrapbook I began long ago. This past week, in cleaning out a cupboard, I found it and began reading some of the stories. When I read the following one, I knew I had received a message. An author, who did not give his name, wrote:

> One afternoon, many years ago, I sat on the front porch of a vine-covered cottage in Hazard, Kentucky. With me was Brother A. S. Petrey, who for over fifty years had been a missionary to the people of the Cumberland Mountains. I asked my friend, "What is the greatest single thing that has happened during your long ministry here?" The grand old preacher did not hesitate. Pointing to a white church building on the hill, he said, "Two Sundays ago I was the guest of honor at the services in that church. As we entered the building, ushers gave each person a red rose. I was taken to the platform and given a seat alongside the pastor.

When the service was almost over, the minister asked me to stand. Then he said, "If Brother
Petrey were responsible for your finding Christ
as your Savior, come up and pin a rose on him."
They started coming from all over the room.
They pinned roses all over me until I looked
like a blooming idiot. But I wouldn't trade those
roses for all the coal, and hardwood, and gold
in all the hills of Kentucky.

Had I been on that porch, I might have given that old
preacher the greatest hug of his life, for I would have known
exactly how great was the gratitude in his soul. It's nice to be
loved; to be remembered. And then, my thoughts ran on. *I
wonder, if I will be remembered after I am gone? And if so, I wonder
what folk will recall when they think of my name.* A chorus in an
old Sankey hymn says, "Only remembered by what we have
done." Probably some people will remember a doctor and say,
"He saved my life." Others will remember a teacher and say,
"She taught me in school." Others might say, "He once was a
neighbor . . . he lived next door." Babe Ruth is remembered
for his skill in baseball, Caruso for his wonderful singing, and
others for military or political achievements. But somehow,
the testimony coming from that old man in Kentucky outshines
them all: "He led me to Christ." Can you imagine what we
would feel in that city where the sun will never set, if someone pointed to us and exclaimed, "He—She—led me to Jesus."
For what will people remember us? Think about it, and lay
up treasure in heaven.

Blessed Are They Who Make Music

T he other morning when I was reading one of Mrs. Charles Cowman's devotional booklets, I was blessed by one of the stories. She described how Sir Michael Costa, the famous conductor, was holding a most important rehearsal. His vast array of musicians and tremendous choir seemed at their best. The mighty chorus rang out with the thunder of organ, sounding horns, and clashing cymbals. Far back in the orchestra, a man who played the piccolo said to himself: "In all this din, it matters not what I do." Then suddenly, all was still. The great conductor flung up his arms and the music stopped. Someone had failed to take his part. The sweet note of the piccolo had been missed. Clearly no one within God's orchestra is unimportant. Sometimes, some of us may think we are, but we are wrong. Even the smallest note of praise is sweet music to our great Leader.

Mrs. Cowman also told of a missionary in China; this man had become so despondent that everything about him seemed touched with sadness. Although he fervently prayed for victory over depression and discouragement, no answer came. Believing he was an utter failure, the man went away to an interior station where he believed he could spend his hours in prayer until victory was assured. When he reached the destination, he was welcomed by the resident missionary and taken into his bedroom in the mission house. Suddenly his soul was gripped by the motto on a card hanging on the wall: *Try Thanksgiving.*

The two words gripped his heart, and he thought to himself, "Have I been praying all these months, and not been praising?" He paused, and then began to praise the Lord for all the blessings he had. Instantly he began to feel better. Instead of hiding away to agonize in prayer, he returned immediately to his waiting converts to tell them that praise changed things. Wonderful blessing followed his simple testimony, and many others were brought into an experience never known before.

As we get closer to Easter, let us remember to praise the Lord. Let us make a joyful noise to the God of our salvation. In our own estimation we may feel very insignificant, but we must never forget that we are intensely precious to God. Instead of looking at the dark side of every cloud, let us look for the silver lining. It is surely there. Never let it be said that heaven's orchestra was hushed because we failed to play our part in the great symphony of praise.

Blessed Are They Who Believe

Many years ago, a man was completely overwhelmed by his problems and suffering. Death appeared to be very near, but in spite of everything, that man, Job, emphatically proclaimed: "For I know that my redeemer liveth, and that he shall stand at the latter day upon the earth. And though . . . worms destroy this body, yet in my flesh shall I see God." I have a feeling that Job would have made an excellent preacher for Easter Sunday. He knew something.

I have often heard my husband and other ministers preaching the Easter message, but I am blessed most when I sit quietly considering the wonderful story of the resurrection. To me, it seems a story of great trust. Simon Peter was adamant in his declaration that God raised Jesus from the dead (Acts 2:24–32). It was no ordinary happening. God himself had stepped into the picture and raised the Lord. But surely the Savior knew it would happen, and with perfect trust laid down his life. It is also a story of such great triumph. That old monster, death, which for so long had seemed invincible, was suddenly and completely conquered. But best of all, it is a story of great truth—a story that needs to be told again and again. Job was sure that in his new body he would see God. We can be just as certain, for we have been told that Christ was but the first fruits of a great harvest. Yes, we must tell this story continually and thereby express our own faith and love. From time to time, our future may appear bleak. We must remember that God is on our side.

I was reading in my scrapbook the other day and found a beautiful story of a man who said that his favorite Bible verse was: "And it came to pass." A friend expressed surprise and pointed out that this was not a verse at all. The man insisted that to him it was even more than a verse—it was everything. He said that in every trouble, problem, and difficulty, he had found comfort in the simple fact that these details came to pass—and not to stay. Oh, if only we could grasp that wonderful truth. It could indeed be the heart of the Easter message for each one of us. If you have a great problem, read Hebrews 12:2 and take heart.

Blessed Are the Palm-tree Christians

Once again Easter is here, and for all who know Christ, it will be a time of great rejoicing. Once again we shall be reminded that our Savior lives; that he triumphed over death, and, thank God, because he lives we shall live also. We live in an astonishing world where scientists can explore outer space and do things previously thought impossible. Yet we know that, great as they are, these same clever men are destined to become shivering old men. Not one of them has yet produced the pill that can defy the ravages of time and banish disease and death. Only Jesus of Nazareth was able to do this, and at this Easter time, we remember and worship.

Palm Sunday is the forerunner of Easter Day, and because I have seen the palm trees growing in many parts of the world, they interest me greatly. The experts tell us that this biblical tree can be used in 360 different ways, but maybe these wise men have failed to see the details that would interest all Christians.

1. The palm tree is a friendly lighthouse in a hot, lonely desert. It is a beacon that beckons travelers to a refreshing oasis.
2. The palm tree supplies shade from the relentless heat of summer days. It is a place of comfort and rest.
3. The palm tree is marvelously reproductive. It sends out runners or suckers that will eventually produce more palms.
4. The palm tree's "fruits" or by-products are multitudinous. The fibrous leaves can be made into fences, rigging, and ropes. Indeed, in New Guinea great bridges over awesome canyons are made entirely of ropes made from the trees. Thus, people who would normally be separated by great gulfs are brought together in fellowship.

It only takes a little imaginative thought to see in all this the simple lesson that we should be as the palm tree. There are many people for whom life resembles a desert. These folk need help. With God's assistance we can guide them to a place of refuge. Our influence might be the shade in which their weary souls will find rest. Perhaps we might even lead them to a saving knowledge of our Lord, and if this be the case, other "palm trees" will begin to appear, and, in miraculous fashion, all our attributes will be rendering service in a world of continuing need.

Probably the palm tree's greatest moment came when its branches were spread at the feet of Jesus on that memorable day when he entered Jerusalem. They occupied the greatest place in all the world.

Blessed Are They Whose Easter Never Ends

The story has often been told how Martin Luther, the great leader of the Reformation, at one period in his life became a victim to despondency. Everything had been very difficult for him, and with opposition increasing daily, the great saint began to lose his joy. His wife was very perplexed about this but hardly knew how lift the clouds from her husband's mind. Then one day she had a great inspiration. Dressing in the deepest black garments, she sorrowfully walked into her husband's room. She must have been a great actress. When Luther looked into her tear-filled eyes, when he saw her grief-stricken face and noticed her mourning apparel, he asked, "Who has died?" She quietly answered, "God is dead." Indignantly Luther replied, "Woman don't talk such nonsense. Who told you such rubbish?" She answered, "You did! God must be dead the way you are carrying on. Yes, he must be dead—really dead." And suddenly Luther's burden lifted. Mrs. Luther must have been a very great lady.

Last Sunday—the first Sunday after Easter, I sat in the church where my husband was to preach and suddenly, as I joined in the responsive reading, the electrifying words "Christ has won" seemed to shine on the page before me. Easter was a beginning and not an end. This is the reason why we should continually give thanks. Through his triumphant resurrection the Lord defeated everything that frustrates us, and now by his living presence, he offers all we need. The glorious songs of Easter should find daily expression in our lives. True thankfulness is a great thing, but surely its child should be praise. We are reminded that in the Jewish temple there were two different kinds of altars. One was for sacrifice, but the other was the place where sweet-smelling incense was burned. The first was necessary because of sin, the other was necessary because grateful sinners, who had found a hiding place, wished to tell God how they felt. We look at Christ's precious blood and feel gratitude. The Lord smells the sweet fragrance and he also feels gratitude, gratitude that he did not die in vain. God rolled back the stone from the door of the tomb. If we now, as Luther did, decide to sit sadly in the shadows, forgetting or ignoring the open door to the sunshine, we are— to say the least—unwise.

If some day you feel under the weather, if everything appears to be going wrong, make time to sit down for ten or fifteen minutes. Then, methodically start thinking about all the nice things that have happened to you during your lifetime. Remember all the blessings that God, from time to time, has made real in your life. I will guarantee that the moment you really start doing this, you will begin to feel better. Our Lord is alive. He cares for us. He watches us. Yes, think on these positive things, and your clouds will disappear. I know it's true.

Blessed Is the God of Little Things

Quite recently, during a visit to a church in California, I picked up a small magazine written especially for children. Its leading article was, "God's Humming Helicopters," and, of course, it referred to hummingbirds. As I read its message, I became very interested, for during certain months of the year, I watch these wonderful creatures feeding outside of our window. Hummingbirds are specially attracted to anything red so we fill our feeding bottles with bright red sugar water, and daily watch these—as one writer described them—"glittering fragments of the rainbows." There are more than five hundred different kinds of hummingbirds; the smallest of all being the fairy hummingbird of Cuba. This particular species is only about two and one-half inches long and holds the world's record for the smallest nest. It is about half the size of a walnut shell! Many hummingbirds are so small that four babies can sit in a teaspoon.

Two of the many kinds of hummers hold an endurance record. They fly at least two thousand miles for their winter vacation, but how they can do it remains a great mystery. The rubythroat, the only hummingbird living in the eastern United States, actually flies nonstop across the Gulf of Mexico. It only weighs about as much as a penny, but it can fly five hundred miles or more without stopping.

To prepare for its long flight, the tiny bird eats enough to double its weight before takeoff. The extra fat provides its needed fuel. All hummingbirds love to eat and average between fifty and sixty meals per day. Naturalists believe they eat half their weight in sugar. If humans needed that much food-energy, they would have to eat 285 pounds of hamburger meat every day! The bird's wings move at the fantastic speed of ninety times per second. During the time it takes us to say, "one thousand and one," a hummingbird will move its wings ninety times. The lovely, lively, little hummingbird teaches us that beauty as well as wisdom is part of God's nature.

If we had to choose between the high flying, majestic golden eagle, and the very tiny fluttering hummingbird, which would we choose? Surely the choice would be very, very difficult. They are both completely fearless, and yet are so different. One specializes in great strength, the other in great speed. Still, God made them both. He is interested in the great things of his world, and just as interested in the tiny things. I candidly admit that this makes me very happy. What if the Lord were only interested in the big things of life and only cared for the great people who steal the limelight and glamour wherever they go? If that were the case, I think most of us would be forgotten. We are such tiny, inconspicuous creatures; we sometimes feel if we were taken away, we would never be missed. Ah, but that would be wrong. He made us, he sees us, and he certainly cares for us—a lot.

Blessed Are They Who Know the Secret

I am sure you that will agree with me when I say that dreams sometimes can be very strange and often very silly. I remember occasions when I awoke after a strange dream to ask myself, "Now where in the wide world did that come from?" At other times, a strange dream has given me much food for thought. I think you will know what I am trying to express.

Not long ago, I heard a Chinese minister telling about a dream with an unusual interpretation of happiness. He told of a man who dreamed and thought he was in hell. He was very surprised to see long tables filled with the most expensive and delicious food, but the people who sat at the tables were most unhappy. Obviously, they were all ravenous and longed to partake of the banquet. They were unable to do so, however, for their arms could not bend at the elbow. Try as they might, they could never bring anything close to their mouths. Their frustration was easy to see. And then, in a moment, the dreamer seemed to be taken to a similar scene in heaven. The tables were covered with the most delicious food, and even the air was filled with bewitching aromas. The people apparently had the same affliction, for their elbows were stiff and unyielding. Yet, they were extremely happy and their

laughter echoed around the room. This was bewildering, and
the dreamer was intrigued. And then he discovered their secret. Although they were unable to feed themselves, they were
able to feed the folk who were sitting opposite them. As they
gave to others, they were also receiving from those they were
helping. And then the dreamer woke to ask himself many
questions.

So often we only think of what we might receive and forget
that the Bible says, "Give, and it shall be given unto you . . .
pressed down, and shaken together, and running over" (Luke
6:38). Long, long ago, two young men in Israel discovered this
great secret, though normally they might have been ruthless
enemies. David and Jonathan became the pattern for true friendship. Jonathan gladly gave up his claim to the throne; in fact, he
gave all he possessed to his young friend, David, but he received infinitely more in return. This new love filling his heart
was something unknown in Saul's palace. It was said of them
that their love surpassed the love of women. Let us try to emu-
late their example. "Then Jonathan and David made a covenant,
because he loved him as his own soul" (1 Sam. 18:3).

Blessed Are They Who Can Make Up Their Minds

Decisions, decisions, decisions. Every day they just crowd in on us, and sometimes they can be exasperating. Not long ago, I heard a woman impatiently complaining about all the decisions that had to be made, and my heart went out to her. It was apparent that frustration was building within her heart, and probably ere the day was through, she would explode. At each and every gas station, drivers have to decide what kind of gas they wish to purchase. People on diets have to decide what foods to eat and what foods to reject. Decisions, decisions, decisions. As my husband says, "They drive you up the wall."

I have just picked up a little devotional book that I have had for many years. At one time or another, I must have written on the inside of the cover, for there I found the words: "For everyone there's a time to decide—that's when the brave man chooses and the coward steps aside." There are moments when it takes real courage to choose for ourselves. Robots do what they are told to do, but God never meant us to be like them. All kinds of pressure is brought to bear on us. Fashion experts tell us what to wear, and some of us spend a lot of hard-earned money buying what we do not need—just because a television commercial influenced our judgment. Happy indeed is the woman who can make up her mind in spite of everything. What we choose oftentimes is a clear indication of what we are. It has been said that one can tell the kind of person by the books he or she reads. And surely, it is possible to recognize a person's taste by the films he or she watches on television. Our decisions as Christians should indicate to all people that we are different. Some folk are apt to yield to the pressure of temptation instead of standing firm for what is obviously right. A little compromise—a little complacency—and soon collapse becomes a reality in the soul. The Bible is filled with stories of men and women who decided for righteousness. When Abram decided for God, he prospered. When he compromised and tried to walk in two directions at the same time, sadness came to his soul. The Bible characters had everything to gain by walking in the path of righteousness. When they decided not to do so, they lost everything. The same thing applies to us. Decisions. We can decide to go to the house of God—or stay at home. We can decide to read the Bible—or watch television. We can decide to resist the Devil—or flirt with him. Pray before you decide anything.

Blessed Are They Who Know How to Use Their Wings

In a recent edition of the *Prairie Overcomer*, the magazine of a wonderful prairie Bible school in Alberta, Canada, the editor wrote of a strange thing that had happened in his country. About ten years ago, the Ontario government's Committee for the Preservation of Wildlife had given a gaggle of geese a home on some land near Owen Sound. There, the birds had all the food they needed, and a wonderful environment in which to live their lives. Normally, as winter comes to the north, these and millions of other birds fly south to warmer climes, but this did not happen with the Owen Sound colony. So much food had made them fat and lazy, and, ultimately, it threatened their existence. The Ontario government flew three hundred of these fat Canadian geese to Florida aboard a Twin Otter aircraft. The birds were too pampered to get there on their own. Commenting on their condition before the flight, one spokesman said: "The geese have no reason to fly away. Right now their food is provided, and they've got it made." This story made me feel a little sad. Sumptuous living had begotten a deadly complacency, and this, in turn undermined the natural strength of the geese. Too much food led to too little exercise. The authorities realized that unless something was done to remedy the situation, the entire plan of preservation would be ruined.

The more I considered this report, the more I became aware of a similar danger in the life of the Christian. The Bible says, "They that wait upon the LORD shall renew their strength; they shall mount up with wings as eagles" (Isa. 40:31). Christians need exercise, not just food. When people are earthbound, they miss the thrill and satisfaction of soaring in nobler and higher realms. Our wings become paralyzed through lack of use. This inevitably leads to danger, for when famine or winter arrives, we have no hidden resources to propel us into the heavens with Christ.

"They that wait upon the Lord"—this seems to be the preparation for flying. Every young pilot is proud when he is able to wear his wings on his chest, but first he has to qualify. And so must we. We wait with eagerness for special television programs, for ball games, for all kinds of earth-born things—but do we wait on the Lord? Too much contentment in Christian service is a threat to our usefulness. In the greatest and most wonderful sense, God made his children able to fly. Happy are they who do so.

Blessed Is the Great Designer

My husband says that the only time he appreciates snow is when he is far removed from it. He has had so many crusades ruined by snow blizzards that now he prefers being a "grease spot" in the desert than a snowman in Canada. But, I do not fully share his thinking. There is something about a storm that is majestic, tremendous, beautiful, and awe inspiring. There have been times when I have been inspired to exclaim, "blessed be the God of the storm." To watch the silent snowflakes drifting serenely to earth and to have one perch cheekily on the tip of one's nose brings a glow of inward satisfaction seldom found. Patrick W. Grace says: "No one who has looked closely at a fallen snowflake can forget the exquisite geometry of it, or its delicacy. Just a chance movement or breath and it is gone." And yet that little visitor in the storm can provide a rare kind of beauty and great insight into the mind of the Creator. By using a plastic resin it is possible to catch and preserve snowflakes for later, more minute study. Patrick Grace says: "Oddly enough, even with the thousands of snowflakes that have been caught and examined, there has never been found any two exactly alike." It is surely interesting to remember that the God who made the vast mountain ranges also designed and made a snowflake. He who made the lark, the song thrush, and the canary also found a place for the raucous crow. Behind his every act is a design of great excellence. Each tiny snowflake is a jewel in disguise, but alas, for the most part, this passes unnoticed. Do you remember the famous lyric, "Catch a falling star and put it in your pocket"? I think it would be even better to catch a falling snowflake and place it in our hearts, for it has something to say to all of us:

1. There is something special about every snow storm. Even if we fail to appreciate the mighty voice of the wind, the beauty of the snowflake is irresistible. Could this also be true of the storms that sometimes seem to devastate our lives? Does God have a purpose and design of which we may be unaware?
2. Beauty is certainly in the heart of the snowflake, but we must pause and search for it. It is very much easier to do nothing but grumble than it is to examine the small treasures a storm might be hiding.
3. If, as do the snowflake collectors, we can preserve our discoveries, they will enrich us forever. We can examine "our snowflakes," and remember that every storm will be filled with similar wonders—all planned by God.

Blessed Are
the Beautiful

Someone has said: "Beauty is in the eye of the beholder." But I feel there is much more to be considered than that simple statement might convey. Another has said that "beauty is only skin deep." That also leaves much to be said. We are now approaching Easter—the time of sacrifice and triumph, and doubtless all over the world people will be thinking of Christ's death and what we might do to express gratitude for his great act. I know a fine young man who asked himself what he could give up during the season of Lent. I was so interested to hear he had decided to give up his beloved cookies. To his developing mind, that was about the greatest sacrifice he could possibly make, for he truly loves cookies. Probably, after Easter, this young lad will make up for lost time. But surely the Lord must love a boy who would do as he is doing, simply to express love to the Christ of Easter.

Do you remember how Mary of Bethany, once she realized that her Master was to die, decided to give to him the best thing she possessed? Somehow, I have always imagined Mary as exceedingly beautiful, but her action of giving her box of precious ointment revealed a beauty of character far beyond that of her radiant face. If loveliness be in the eyes of the beholder, then the Lord's eyes must be pools of delight each time he sees a devoted servant. How he appreciates the dedication of his followers. Our lives should emit a fragrance that comes just from him, for it is only in this way that we succeed in reaching the people among whom we live.

The other day, I read an old Chinese proverb that said: "The sandalwood tree imparts its fragrance even to the ax which cuts it down." This was certainly true of the Lord, for one of the soldiers who crucified him said afterward, "Truly this was the Son of God." It was also true of Stephen, for when he was being stoned to death, something marvelous reached out to grip and change the life of Saul of Tarsus, as he was standing by, watching.

Many years ago, I read of a small boy who wondered why his mother always wore gloves. One day he watched her as she was washing her hands, and he saw terrible scars that he had never seen before. She told him that when he had been a baby, his life had been threatened by a fire that had swept through their home. She had been badly burned as she risked her life to save him. Through tear-filled eyes, the child saw those scarred hands and said, "Oh mother, your hands are beautiful." It is generally easy to love the good and the lovely, but when we understand and go the second and third mile to love even the unlovely, then truly the beauty of Jesus shines in us.

Blessed Are They Who Shine Where They Are

I have known many people who looked with longing eyes toward the far-away mission field. They sighed and thought, *If only I could be there to work for Christ*. I have watched young people who sat spellbound in a service as the preacher expounded the Word of God. Afterward, I listened as they asked all kinds of questions about how they could become great preachers. So many want to be important and in the limelight, and yet, alas, they are not so enthusiastic about working where they are.

Recently, I read a fable about a little lost piece of glass—of its heartbreak, disappointment, frustration, and finally, its resolve. It was said that an artist, in the midst of preparing stained glass for a very important cathedral window, inadvertently knocked a small piece of glass from his bench. Unnoticed, the little lost treasure lay in the dust and wondered what would become of it. The artist seemed preoccupied with bigger and better pieces of the window, and, feeling forgotten and alone, the small piece of glass sighed in the dirt of the floor. But then

61

one day, this little fellow—if I may call him by that name—
realized that he was meant to shine anyhow. To sit there longing for grander moments would only be a waste of precious
time. So, in spite of the unattractiveness of his surroundings,
the small piece of glass decided to get on with his job of shining. When a ray of sunshine came down from the window,
the glass seemingly smiled, and this flash of brilliance attracted
the attention of the artist. He stopped and lifted the lost treasure from the dust. He had specially planned that this should
be the "eye" of Christ in the soon-to-be famous window.
Gently, carefully, the artist placed the glass where it was meant
to be, and ever afterward people who gazed up into the face
of the Savior found help and comfort from what they saw.
They often said: "He seems to be looking at me."

It is a law of the Christian life that, if we are faithful in the
small things, God will promote us to greater realms of service.
If we are content and willing to shine just where we are, even
though it be a dirty old corner of a dusty floor, the Great Artist
will see us and gently lift us up to do what all along he had
prepared us to do. The true joy of service is to shine where we
are. Maybe some who read these words will feel that they are
in a most undesirable corner. "Oh, if only I could get out." If
God wants us in a larger and more glamorous place, he can
and will take us to it. Our present sphere might be the prepara-
tory ground for bigger and better things. Don't pine—shine.
You may be sure that his eye will recognize the radiance.

Blessed Are the Fire-bird Christians

A few years ago, I accompanied my husband to Arizona and made my first visit to the city of Phoenix. I had not been there long before someone gave me an official brochure about the district, and as I read its contents, suddenly, I became vitally interested. Let me explain why.

The first people to settle in the Phoenix area were Hohokam Indians. They diverted the water of the Salt River into a complex network of irrigation ditches and several of these narrow canals are still being utilized today. However, what became of the Hohokam Indians is a mystery. Later, when thirty settlers came to live in the district, there arose the need for a name for the location. Darrell Duppa suggested a mythical name that was unanimously accepted. He told an ancient story. To the Egyptians, the phoenix bird had been a symbol of immortality. They believed that every five hundred years this bird set itself afire only to rise again from its own ashes. Duppa, an educated Englishman, suggested the imaginative name of Phoenix for that place, because five hundred years before, the entire Hohokam tribe had disappeared. They left only their canals behind, and these were to become the arteries—the pulse beat—of this new settlement.

Doubtless, the idea behind the name was that the Indians had died only to rise again in a new form. Their death led to a resurrection beyond their wildest dreams. The great city of Phoenix is today their unspoken testimony. People die only to live again.

"I am crucified . . . nevertheless, I live," said Paul, and this seems to be the pathway to blessedness. The leaves of a tree will die in the fall, only to reappear in all the beauty of spring. The corn of wheat will be buried in the ground only to reappear in the golden grain waving serenely in the summer breeze. It seems to be a law of life: we die to live, we give, and yet gain; we kneel, and somehow grow taller every day. We make time to speak often with God, and then our labors become far more effective. I cannot help but think of the widow of Zarephath who gave her very last meal to Elijah only to discover that afterward, "the barrel of meal wasted not, neither did the cruse of oil fail, according to the word of the LORD, which he spake by Elijah" (1 Kings 17:16). Read the story. It is marvelous. In contrast, let me tell a story that one of my friends often tells. A little boy was given two dimes. One was for the Lord, to be placed in the collection at church; the other was for candy. On the way to church, the lad slipped on the street. One of the dimes fell from his hand and rolled down the street drain. The lad looked at the solitary remaining dime, and then, lifting his eyes toward the sky, he said, "I'm sorry, Lord."

Hitler boasted, "What we have, we hold," and he lost all. God says, "What you give, you never lose"—even though, like the fire bird, it may be lost to us for a while.

Blessed Is the God Who Arranges Things

To some of my readers, what I have to relate might seem commonplace, but I have long since learned that we see God best in the little things of life. People do tell marvelous stories of great miracles performed. But somehow, I like to see the hand of the Lord arranging the tiniest of details. During a recent tour, something happened in Rome and Greece that I shall remember forever.

One of our very dear friends on a previous tour had taken many photographs, but these had never been made into the slides so necessary for visual presentations in a church service. The next year, he returned with his wife, and a very special and expensive camera. He had great plans and was as excited as a school boy facing a new adventure. In Rome, that intricate camera jammed and it seemed beyond repair. My friend telephoned back to America in the hope that some advice might help. Alas, nothing could be done. What a disappointment! Everybody else was getting excellent pictures, but he was getting none. It was so easy to recognize the intense frustration in our brother's face. His trip was being spoiled.

The desk clerk in the hotel in Greece said he understood cameras, but the job was too great for him. He did know, however, the address of a firm that handled these expensive cameras. The next morning, my husband went with our friend to the place, only to be told, "We can do it, but not today." We now know that the young man skilled in handling these complicated cameras had been called to military service, and without his help, the firm could do little. The situation seemed hopeless, but still the owner of the shop promised to try. Later, thank God, the young expert, dressed in his army uniform, walked into the shop. Apparently, he had a day off and had decided to visit his employer. When our friend went back at noon, his camera was waiting for him. Thereafter, he was able to "shoot up a storm." Now all this may not seem a great deal to a casual reader, but as I have already stated, I have learned to look for the Lord in the little things of life. I cannot help but marvel that the young man should walk into a shop where his help was so urgently needed.

Yes, God is our heavenly Father, and he really does care for his own. The Lord said that not even a sparrow could fall to the ground unnoticed. Then he told his disciples that they were of more value than many sparrows. Sometimes I forget that truth, and then he says: "Oh ye of little faith." Isn't God good?

Blessed Are They Who Can Be Still

We seem to be living in a crazy world. The rush, the tension, and the strain are proving too great for people. Events that have taken place in the world during the last few years only prove what I am saying. And right in the middle of all the frenzied activities stands the housewife. Meals have to be cooked, children reared, dishes washed, and no sooner has one lot been handled, then another stares us in the face. Telephones ring, people come to our doors, supermarkets have to be visited, provisions bought, and when we have seemingly finished, we remember some other important task that escaped us. Then somebody asks, "What do you do with your time?"

Maybe the psalmist knew something about this, for one day in the midst of it all, he heard the Lord say, "Be still, and know that I am God" (Ps. 46:10). But then comes the question, "How can I be still when I have so much to do?" I know that this is a very hard lesson, but we must learn it. Without it, life becomes intolerably difficult. I shall never forget how, after a major surgery some years ago, my wonderful doctor said to me, "There will be times when you will feel terrible. You may be in the middle of washing dishes—anything, when suddenly, without warning, you will feel as if you are about

to drop. When this happens, you must leave everything and
go lie down for half an hour. If you do this, you will be all
right." I soon learned that the doctor was correct. I have also
found out that the same rules apply in my spiritual life. There
are times when we must leave what we are doing and go aside
to be still. I also believe that we never really know God until
we take the time to be still. The Lord gives us little warnings,
and if we heed his voice, we are able to weather the storms
that break over our heads. If we do not obey his whispered
command, we are soon overwhelmed. Then it is so easy to
become irritable and say things we never really mean. The
tension can mount until even the sun seems to have been
eclipsed. "Be still, my soul—thy God is on the throne." So
wrote the hymnist.

Do you remember how, at the Red Sea, when people were
beginning to complain, when danger threatened from all sides,
and when Israel seemed about to be overwhelmed, Moses said,
"Fear ye not, stand still, and see the salvation of the LORD"
(Exod. 14:13). It is so hard to stand when your heart says, "Run
for your life." It is so hard to be still when everything around
us and within us suggests we are about to go under. Yet, if
God be on the throne, and if he sees me, am I really in danger?
Jesus said of the sparrows, that "one shall not fall on the ground
without your Father. . . . Fear not therefore, ye are of more
value than many sparrows" (Matt. 10:29, 31). Be still my soul,
the Lord is on your side. Think about it.

Blessed Are They Who Find the Pearl of Great Price

During a recent stay in Belgium, I was fascinated by a story told by Robert Barr. In one of his books, he wrote about the daughters of a famous Roman general whose name was Stilicho. These illustrious young ladies died in the year A.D. 407. As was the custom in those days, their precious jewels were buried with them. Today, it is difficult for modern people to understand the wisdom of such an act. Archaeologists have uncovered tombs in which enormous treasures were buried with the bodies of their owners. Indeed, the grave robbers of ancient times often became wealthy plunderers. The story of the Stilicho wealth was handed down from generation to generation and many unsuccessful attempts were made to find the tomb. No one succeeded until the year 1526. When the tomb was opened, the jewels were discovered undamaged and intact. The pearls, unfortunately, had lost their luster owing to centuries of being buried in the darkness. This was the one disappointing feature about the accomplishment. The pearls, which had once been a treasure of incalculable worth, had become utterly worthless.

I remembered how Matthew wrote of man who found "a pearl of great price," and to possess it completely, he sold all that he had (Matt. 13:46). Throughout the history of the church, many sermons have been preached about this Pearl of Great Price—the Lord Jesus Christ. All the riches of an eternal world were represented in him. He, too, was buried, but thank God, he did not remain in the tomb until the luster had diminished. He rose again, and his glory still shines with an unrivaled brilliance. Happy indeed is the person who finds this Pearl.

The more I think of this, the more the story appeals to me. I would like to preach about it. Wouldn't you?

1. Real pearls are not easily found—they have to be sought. They are formed through suffering, when a grain of sand somehow gets inside the shell of an oyster. Not all shells contain a pearl. Those who seek them must be persistent.
2. Real pearls are valuable—they more than compensate for any effort or sacrifice made in the search. Even the search can be exciting if one's eyes see the beautiful possibilities instead of the dirty shells. Without the smelly shells, the sand, and the mud, pearls would not even exist.
3. Real pearls, in days gone by, suggested a palace, a kingdom, a crown—for only royalty could afford them.

Yet, such a treasure comes to us as a gift from heaven. Blessed are they who find . . .

Blessed Are the Sheep

Some years ago, my sister came with her husband from Wales to visit us in Santa Barbara. This was the first time she had left her native country, and I am happy to be able to say, she fell in love with America. We were able to take them to many places of interest, but perhaps, after Disneyland, the best was the San Diego Zoo. There we saw almost every kind of animal, bird, and reptile, but at the time of our visit, I hardly thought of comparing the place with a church. Now, I have just read an article written by J. Harold Smith, and my mind is working overtime. He writes,

> Would you vote to turn the church into a zoo? I am sure such a thing could never get a passing vote in any church business meeting. But what about your own personal vote?

> Some members are as stubborn as a Missouri Mule about doing church work, but as sly as a Fox in their own business deals; as busy as a Bee in spreading the latest gossip, but as quiet as a Mouse in spreading the gospel of Christ. Many are as blind as a Bat to see the needs of others,

7 1

but have the eyes of a Hawk to see the faults of a few. Some are eager as a Beaver about a barbecue, but as lazy as a Dog about the prayer meeting. Some will roar like a Lion when things do not suit them, but they are as gentle as a Lamb when they need the preacher of the church. Some are as noisy as a Blue Jay when calling on the church for advice, but as timid as a Kitten about talking to the lost, and as slow as a Snail about visiting absentees and shut-ins. Many are Night Owls on Saturday night, hibernating Bears on Sunday morning, slippery as Eels on Sunday evenings, and as scarce as Hen's teeth on Wednesday nights. Yet, with such a collection of Zoo Members, they expect the church to grow, build new buildings, pay all the bills, and jump every time they whine or let out a bellow.

Thank God for the *Sheep Members*. They are the ones who furnish the wool, milk, and meat of God's house. They are a joy to the preacher's heart and an honor to the Name of our God.

Mr. Smith's list could be lengthened quite a lot. Have we not all known members as changeable as a chameleon, as snappy as a turtle, as frightening as a charging bull, as dangerous as a stalking leopard, and as talkative as a parrot?

Blessed are the sheep. Our Lord said: "My sheep hear my voice, and I know them, and they follow me: And I give unto them eternal life: and they shall never perish" (John 10:2–28). To recognize his blessed voice, to walk in his footsteps, to receive life everlasting from his outstretched hand; these are the vital qualities in life. Perhaps the Lord could have called some of us by the name of another animal, but he preferred to call us sheep. I am glad he did. There is something so attractive about a lamb, and something so warm and inviting about an old sheep.

Happy, so happy is the person who can say, "The LORD is my Shepherd. I shall not want. He maketh me to lie down in green pastures; he leadeth me beside the still waters." I am so glad that our wonderful Lord is my Shepherd.

Blessed Is
the Polished Shaft

All our friends know that we had a room full of seashells in our home. Each shell was an object of great beauty, and our visitors appeared to be fascinated as we explained the history of the varying specimens. Some shells were rugged and plain, but others were so pretty they almost begged description. Yet, they all came out of the ocean and were formed amid similar conditions. The same kind of winds, rocks, sand, waves, and storms all played a part in the creative skill of the mollusk that patiently made its shell home. The ruggedness of certain shells provided the creature's strong defense against its enemies, but almost without exception, our visitors were more attracted to the polished shells. The colors were so integrated and blended, the gloss so unbelievably beautiful that they were truly magnificent.

Yesterday, I was thinking about this and the text from Isaiah 49:2 came into my mind. "In the shadow of his hand hath he hid me, and made me a polished shaft." I could almost see the prophet as he slowly turned the polished arrow in his hand. His eyes surely sparkled as certain thoughts became more and more clear.

1. It had lain in its owner's hand; it had been very, very near to him.
2. It had been the object of patient, loving care and had received special attention. No arrow could become polished without this.
3. When finished, it was a source of great pride to the man who had worked on it.
4. It was most effective, for it could penetrate where other arrows could not.

And as Isaiah examined his polished arrow, he must have wondered as I do: How many of God's people are polished shafts? Have you ever watched the television ads depicting a woman polishing her dining table? Did you see the ad of the housewife who sees her face reflected in the shine on her washed dishes? We are constantly reminded that it takes something very special to produce such a polish. Isaiah knew this long before television was discovered. He said: "In the shadow of his hand hath he hid me." That is where the polishing is done.

Some of us, as shells, may be tumbled around by all kinds of waves, but the buffeting may assist in the polishing process.

It has often been said that entering the armed services will either make or break a young man, but the same may be said of all the problems of life. It is always disappointing to see a woman or a man who has become embittered by circumstances. Yet, others seem to develop through adversity a tenderness, a radiance, a charm that is irresistible. A polished arrow is an object of pride to its owner. I wonder: *Is the Lord proud of me?* Is it easy for him to see his face in the gloss on my life? I have known people who measured up to these exalted standards, and their lives were really beautiful. Being in their presence for a few moments was all that was necessary to know that they rested in the shadow of the Almighty. The grace of God had been imprinted on their souls and had produced heavenly beauty.

Blessed Are
the Glowworms

Many years ago, the wife of the minister in whose church we were holding special meetings, took me to the famous glowworm colony in the Waitomo Caves in New Zealand. I shall never forget what I saw and learned that day. After a short walk through the various caves, we climbed into a small boat and were told to remain very quiet. The boat was pulled along by a rope already in position; we were in complete darkness. Suddenly, we entered the famous cave, and the sight was unbelievable. Millions of glowworms, clinging to the roof of the very spacious cavern, were letting their lights shine. Our guide had already explained that if we made the slightest sound, all the lights would go out. We therefore sat in silence and marveled at the beautiful blue radiance illuminating the roof of the cave. It was gorgeous; supremely wonderful, and yet to us, who had seen so many things, it was just another tourist attraction. Then I thought of something. I remembered what the guide had said: "It is impossible for the glowworm to turn off its light for long periods without dying. Its light must shine if it expects to live." Moreover, one little glow-worm shining alone would be unnoticed, but millions shining together could light a cave. In the same way it might be true to say that one insignificant Christian shining alone might not appear too effective, but when millions of us unite, our joint efforts can illuminate the world. The message I heard in that cave so many years ago is still with me. If, as Christians, we expect to live—we must let our light shine. It is impossible to stay in the dark for long periods of time *without dying*. And we must shine together to make a good light for the Lord.

Letting our lights shine before others does not necessarily mean preaching or testifying by word of mouth to our friends. Our light can shine in various ways. For example, on one occasion people gathered to pray for a family known to be in great financial need. While one of the deacons offered a fervent prayer, there was a loud knock on the door. When someone responded, there in the doorway stood the sturdy son of one of the local farmers. "What do you want, boy?" asked one of the elders. The lad replied, "Pa couldn't come, so he asked me to bring his prayers in the wagon." "What do you mean?" asked the astonished churchman. "As I said," continued the lad, "I brought Pa's prayers in the wagon. Just come out and help me, and we'll bring them in." Pa's prayers consisted of potatoes, flour, beef, oatmeal, turnips, apples, jellies, and clothing. The prayer meeting adjourned on short notice.

Do you have a grumpy old neighbor? Or a hard-to-please, irritable husband? Or stubborn, rebellious children? Or whatever? Let your light shine. A smile is always better than a frown. A hand outstretched to assist is always of more value than a punch. Sometimes this may seem difficult, but remember the glowworm—if you want to live.

Blessed Are They Who Spread the Faith

Recently, as I was examining our mail, I saw that a very special sticker was attached to one of the envelopes. The message so vividly portrayed read: Don't *keep* the Faith, *spread it*. Instantly, my thoughts went back to the Holy Land, as, in memory, I stood by the banks of the River Jordan. I remembered how John the Baptist had been there, faithfully spreading the good tidings. His faithfulness led to a great harvest of souls. A seed on a shelf will probably wither and die. One seed planted might germinate and grow but would never accomplish very much. But countless seeds scattered into fertile soil might mean the difference between life and death for the hungry. People have always recognized this fact, and thus, from the beginning of time, farming has been an honorable, though difficult, profession.

Many years ago in Africa, my husband and I watched a man slowly walking across a field, seemingly playing a violin. His left hand held the instrument under his chin; his right hand methodically drew the bow back and forth. Actually he was spreading seed. Each time he pushed the bow to its limit, he scattered seeds to a distance of about three feet. His task seemed endless. During earlier visits to the Holy Land, in the

Arab territories, we often saw farmers sowing seeds right and left as they walked over the fields. Today, in more developed countries, it is possible to see elaborate machines doing that job. What used to take many weeks, can now be completed in hours. Such is the age in which we live. Yet, the truth is still unchanging—seed must be spread.

Do you remember how a few years ago many Christians in the southern states had a slogan they used on every possible occasion: *Keep the faith, baby*. Of course, with some people this referred to politics, and sometimes it was a battle cry for those who were engaged in civil rights reform. We heard it on the radio and on television; we read it in the newspapers, and, ultimately, it became commonplace. Now somebody has a new slogan: *Don't keep it, spread it*. Whatever motivated the thought, it seems good to me.

It is written that after the death of Stephen, the Christians "that were scattered abroad went every where preaching the word" (Acts 8:4). If they had been concerned only with their safety, they would have fled to new localities, tried to find employment, and as orderly citizens, merged with the local inhabitants. Had they done this, their consciences would have tormented them. They were in possession of the Good Seed— the Word of God—and they had to spread it or disappoint their Lord. He had given the Great Commission: "Go ye into all the world, and preach the gospel" (Mark 16:15). They dared not fail him. Their faithfulness gave birth to churches all over the world. Today, let us spread the faith.

Blessed Is the God of Surprises

The longer I live, the more convinced I am that God loves to surprise His children. Often we pray for the great things in life, and when our answers arrive, we rejoice for the moment but soon take them for granted. If I might borrow my husband's words: "I think God gets a bigger 'kick' out of things when he is able to see amazement on the face of his child at totally unexpected blessings." For example:

The customs shed in New York was an absolute madhouse. Our plane from Belgium had arrived late; our plane for Los Angeles was soon to leave, and between the two stood the long line of people waiting to have their bags examined. Beyond that line, there was a long ride in the airport bus to the new terminal. The outlook was very dismal, for it seemed certain we could not get through the hassle in time. Hundreds of suitcases were all over the floor; everybody was pushing this way and that, and well, it *was* a madhouse. My spouse went to find a pushcart to transport luggage to the customs bench, and I could only stand and watch helplessly. And then it happened. From nowhere came an official to ask me, "Madam, can I help you? Is anybody helping you?" I wondered who he was, but then I recognized his uniform. He was a senior customs officer. I thanked him and explained that my husband had gone to find a cart for the luggage. At that moment, my husband returned with the bags. The man looked at the cart, asked a few questions, and took us through the gates without any examination whatsoever. Then he said, "We always like to help the elderly." I looked at him, smiled, and forgave him. By this time, my husband had really awakened. He asked another official if he could go back through the gates to help his party members and the person replied: "No."

So, not to be outdone, my husband went to another gate, without permission went through to find our benefactor, and asked if he would be so kind as to help three others of our party. He did so, and by the time they came through, we had someone waiting to take their baggage. The journey to the other terminal seemed painfully slow, but eventually we made it. When my husband ran ahead to ask if the officials would hold the plane a few minutes, the man at the gate refused to cooperate. Nevertheless, we rushed through security and scampered onto the plane. I sat down and, even before I could fasten my seatbelt, the plane was being towed out of its stall. As the proverbial saying goes, we had all made it by the skin of our teeth. Before we could get our breath back, we were airborne. It all happened so quickly, so unexpectedly.

Afterward, as we flew through the skies, I recognized that, but for the stranger who came from nowhere to help, we would have been stranded in New York. Now why did that official come to *me*, when so many others were standing around? I like to feel that God was watching and maybe laughing. He knew exactly what he was going to do for us that day. He had his man ready. Isn't God wonderful?

Blessed Are They Who Go as Far as They Can

Have you ever felt sorry for a baby bird struggling hard to break its way out of a shell? Have you ever been tempted, as I have, to help the struggling infant? Yet God has so ordered that this struggle strengthens the baby and prepares it for life in the world it is about to enter. Without the initial difficulties, the bird might never be able to live its life. This is also true in our world. Recently, I have been deriving much help from Vance Havner's devotional book *Day by Day*. In one passage, he has brought two texts together: "they saw that the stone was rolled away" (Mark 16:4) and "take ye away the stone" (John 11:39). The Bible teaches that there are things that we are expected to do, and there are things that only God can do for us. Blessed is the person who goes as far as possible and then has the faith to leave the rest with the Lord.

When Jesus came to the tomb of Lazarus, doubtless he could have spoken a word and that stone would have moved. Yet, he chose not to do this. He told those present to do what they could. He was wise. We should never ask the Lord to do our work. Nevertheless, some things are beyond our strength, and in contemplating these problems, we are so prone to worry and worry and worry.

The women who went to the tomb on that resurrection morning had the same problem. They said, "Who shall roll us away the stone from the door of the sepulcher?" And when they looked, they saw that it had already been moved. Most of our problems appear to be of the same kind—very great. They loom like specters ahead of us, and we are quite sure we shall never be able to handle them. The women at the tomb discovered that the angel had arrived ahead of them. Well, he always does, but we never discover that blessed fact until— as did the women—we go as far as we can.

Doubt says, "Whatever shall I do?" Faith replies, "God will be there and will do it for me." If, as a baby chick, we are allowed to struggle just a little, it must surely be that we need a little exercise and strengthening. It is a case of "he knoweth the way that I take: when he has tried me, I shall come forth as gold" (Job 23:10).

Our forefathers knew this truth. They tilled the soil, planted their corn, went as far as they could, and then lifted their eyes unto the hills from whence came their aid. We should remember the same wonderful truths.

Blessed Are They Who Begin at the Beginning

A British officer was stationed with his battalion in Madras during very hot and oppressive weather. He lay on his bed thinking of the news he had heard: Hebich is coming. He was a little apprehensive, for Samuel Hebich was a missionary.

Suddenly, a very tall, strange-looking man entered the tent. He had a loose-hanging coat, a huge hat, and a still larger umbrella. He was a sight to cause laughter. Yet, his dignified face and penetrating eyes spoke of tenderness, kindness, and sympathy. The officer felt embarrassed even in his own tent. Calmly, Hebich took a seat and said, "Get down the Book."

The man knew what Book was needed, and though he never read the Bible, he possessed a copy and went to get it.

Hebich continued, "Open the Book at the first chapter of Genesis and read the first two verses."

The officer obeyed, and read: "In the beginning God created the heaven and the earth. And the earth was without form and void. And darkness was upon the face of the deep. And the Spirit of God moved upon the face of the waters."

Hebich said, "That will do. Now close the Book and we will pray." They knelt as the missionary prayed. Then the strange visitor solemnly shook hands and left. The following day, Hebich came again and repeated what he had done earlier. When he prayed, he implored God to open the officer's eyes, then he again departed, leaving the open Bible on the table.

Left alone, the young man was very upset and somehow felt drawn to read again the same two verses. He read them over and over until they seemed to burn in his being. Yes, he was void, darkness was upon the face of his soul. The next day he heard again the footsteps of Hebich, but this time he was ready for the missionary. He blurted out, "Oh Mr. Hebich, it is now plain to me. What must I do?"

The missionary said, "My son, we hear that God said, 'Let there be light.' Believe on the Lord Jesus Christ and thou shalt be saved." When they knelt to pray this time, the officer, for the first time in his life without a book, prayed from his heart to thank the One who had saved him. That British officer was the grandfather of Lieutenant General Sir William Dobbie, one of the greatest of all British generals, and the heroic defender of Malta during World War II. Captain G. S. Dobbie of the Africa Evangelistic Band was another grandson. Did Samuel Hebich realize all that would follow when he began at the beginning?

Who knows what the final result may be in any service we try to do in the Lord's name. I am impressed by the fact that Hebich went away—twice—and allowed the Holy Spirit to have a chance in the man's life. So often we try to do it all.

Happy indeed is the man or woman who knows when to speak and when to bow gracefully out of the picture so that Christ may have the preeminence. It is evident that Mr. Hebich had walked that road himself, and therefore he knew how to lead the officer along the same path. Happy shall we be if we follow that example.

Blessed Are They Who Can Laugh

One day a church bulletin from Florida arrived at our home, and under the heading, "Pastor's Paragraphs" was the following letter. It was entitled, "Miracles Do Happen." It went as follows:

> Attendance at church last Sunday was mighty poorly. I don't reckon I oughta grumble 'cause I had a bunch of sick members, and when you add all that to the shut-ins, we don't have an over lot of pew-fillers. So I went ahead and preached what I had. Only thing was the echo of the near empty church hurt my head. It done the trick alright. What I saw made me rejoice. I saw a miracle after miracle. Ole Hezekiah, who had been deathly ill that morning had roused up and was riding down the highway with his fishing poles. No, nothing but a miracle could have rescued old Hez from the jaws of death in such a short time.
>
> Then there's Rufe's brother. Rufe told me Sunday morning that his brother's back was

in foul shape and they were afraid an operation was gonna be necessary. Well, we remembered him in our prayers, and lo and behold, at two o'clock, there he stood at the driving range, hitting golf balls. If that wasn't a quick recovery, I don't know what is. All told, about twenty of my sick folk roused up and were taking nourishment in one form or another. But what made me really happy was to see so many of my shut-ins riding round enjoying the world. Hez's paw, who don't attend church 'cause he can't stand crowds, was heading for the drag races. Sister Nell's mama, who was too weak to come out of the house, was in town shopping. Ellie Nicklesinger's sister, who can't come out on account of her kidneys, stood in line two hours to get into the show. It was called *The Miracle Worker*. I thought it was right appropriate seeing as how a miracle had happened to her.

Yes sir, it thrilled my heart to see what I saw. I ought to have a packed house next Sunday with all the sick folks healed and all the shut-ins set free. I just hope they don't overdo themselves before next Sunday and have a relapse. I gotta go now and play with my youngest young-un.

Blessed are they who can laugh. It would hardly be possible to read the comments of that quaint pastor without smiling. At least, in addition to its suggestive comments, it proves there are always two ways of looking at things. Sometimes circumstances are so depressing that it would be easy to feel the entire world is against us and that all our work is in vain. And then, a sudden change of outlook, a new slant on things, and a miraculous patch of blue begins to appear in the very center of our cloudy skies. Yes, God showed great wisdom when he made us capable of laughing. There is nothing really attractive about a long, solemn face. Grim straight lips and patches of blue beneath the eyes are somewhat repelling, but sparkling eyes, ripples of mirth, and an overflowing joyful heart are irresistible. Resolve today that you will make someone smile. It's catching.

Blessed Is the God
of the Cul-de-sacs

New Zealand is perhaps the most wonderful of all the countries my husband and I have ever visited. It appears to have everything, including the most wonderful, yet frustrating cul-de-sacs. There are highways that lead to some of the most scenic places in the world; there are others that lead nowhere. For many years, the greatest of the latter kind led to an impassable range of mountains. Beyond these great hills lies the unbelievable splendor of Milford Sound. From the waters of this bay, Mitre Peak lifts its head five thousand feet into the air, and spectacular walls of rock rise straight up from the sea. Not too long ago, the only access to this wonderland was by sea, and tourists would pay a lot of money to sail around the southernmost point of the country just to see this wonder of God's handiwork. The other side of the hill was the annoying cul-de-sac where one could see nothing. Then, the New Zealand government decided something had to be done to change the matter. At great cost, they tunneled through the mountains so that visitors could take the shortcut to, what many called, paradise. The recent gas shortage reminded me of the only time we visited this place. We were informed that gasoline could be obtained at one and only one station just before the mountain, but when we arrived, the owner had

gone to meet a relative and the pump was locked. My husband had to walk nine miles to get gas. But for the fact that
the government had by then turned the cul-de-sac into a highway, he might have been walking forever.

It is so nice to remember that God can turn our cul-de-sacs
into highways leading to blessedness. Do you remember the
account of Israel facing the Red Sea? In front of them, the water; on either side, the mountains; and behind, the advancing
army of Pharaoh. There appeared to be no way out. And then
Moses stretched out his hand over the sea and God opened a
new highway (see Exod. 14:14–31).

> Got any rivers you think are uncrossable?
> Got any mountains you can't tunnel through?
> God specializes in things thought impossible,
> He can accomplish what you cannot do.

It is interesting to notice that God led his people into that
cul-de-sac because *he knew exactly what he intended to do*. The
children of Israel were very shortsighted; they saw only the
problems, and alas, we are so like them. Do you remember
the three Hebrew boys who were cast into the burning fiery
furnace? That surely was the hottest dead end they had ever
imagined, but God turned it into a highway on which they
met one like unto the Son of God. Some of life's choicest
lessons are learned in the most unattractive schools, and happy
indeed is the student who looks, not at the immediate surroundings—but into the face of the Teacher. I cannot help but
wonder if some of you have reached one of life's cul-de-sacs.
Does it appear there is no way out of your problems? Look up.

Blessed Are They Whose Hearts Vibrate

Whenever I am alone I love to read, for books can open up new worlds. Some time ago, I discovered a famous mystery story that was written around the idea of sympathetic vibrations. A very valuable violin had been stolen, but the detective in charge of the investigation believed it was hidden somewhere near the scene of the robbery. The thief had obviously been surprised and had had to escape in a hurry without his treasure. Assuming that in his haste the man had had no time to loosen the strings of the priceless stolen violin, the detective walked back and forth through the building vigorously bowing the strings of another violin. At intervals, he would stop suddenly to quiet the vibrations of his own instrument while he stood listening. Eventually he was rewarded when he heard the quiet tones and sympathetic vibrations coming from the stolen violin that had been locked in a hidden cabinet. As I have indicated, the entire story was woven around the vibrations of the two instruments. The hidden one responded to the sounds of the other.

Paul writes in Romans 8:16: "The Spirit itself beareth witness with our spirit, that we are the children of God." Sometimes it is extremely difficult to explain this to a non-Christian.

Nevertheless, all who know the Savior are aware of the spiritual responses that arise from the soul whenever the Lord speaks. Paul also said that the natural man could not understand the things of the Spirit, and this we know to be true, but Christians understand. God has been pleased to implant in us the ability to respond to him whenever he calls. Perhaps this suggests, therefore, that he always knows where to find us. We can never be completely lost. A well-known hymn says, "Down in the human heart, crushed by the Tempter, feelings lie buried that grace can restore." Happy indeed is the person who takes time to pause within the daily routine just to listen. Was that what the Lord meant when he said, "Be still and know that I am God"? I often think of the experiences of Elijah after he had run away from Jezebel. His life had been devastated by the turmoil of his times, but eventually he reached the solitude of a hillside cave where, utterly weary, he lay down to sleep. After an earthquake and a fire, there came a still small voice. "And it was so, when Elijah heard it, that he wrapped his face in his mantle, and went out, and stood in the entering in of the cave. And, behold, there came a voice unto him, and said, 'What doest thou here, Elijah?'" (1 Kings 19:13). The prophet certainly ran away from Jezebel, but he soon discovered that no one can run away from God—we can neither run far enough nor fast enough. The Lord knew exactly where to find the prophet, and he knows exactly where to find us. But the thing that impresses me most is not that he knows how, where, and when to find us, but rather that he *wants* to find us. We are of more value than a million violins. If you can hear his voice, he cannot be far away.

Blessed Are They Who Do Not Worry

Y ears ago, I was enthralled as I listened to a pastor who for several years had faithfully served the church. His executive responsibilities had taken him all over this country. As he concluded his message, he told of one of the most frightening yet thought-provoking experiences of his life. He had been on a long flight from one place to another. The first warning of the approaching problems came when the sign on the airplane flashed on: Fasten your seatbelts. Then, after a while, a calm voice said, "We shall not be serving the beverages at this time as we are expecting a little turbulence. Please be sure your seatbelt is fastened." As he looked around the aircraft, it was obvious that many of the passengers were becoming apprehensive. Later, the voice of the announcer said, "We are so sorry that we are unable to serve the meal at this time. The turbulence is still ahead of us." And then the storm broke. The ominous cracks of thunder could be heard even above the roar of the engines. The jagged forked lightening lit up the darkened skies, and within moments that great plane was like a cork tossed around on a celestial ocean. One moment the airplane was lifted on terrific currents of air; the next, it dropped as if it were about to crash. The pastor confessed that he shared the discomfort and fear of those around him.

He said, "As I looked around the plane, I could see that nearly all the passengers were upset and alarmed. Some were praying. The future seemed ominous, and many were wondering if we would make it through the storm. And then, I suddenly saw a little girl. Apparently the storm meant nothing to her. She had tucked her feet beneath her as she sat on the seat; she was reading a book, and everything within her small world was calm and orderly. Sometimes she closed her eyes; then she would read again; then she would straighten her legs, but worry and fear were not in her world. When the plane was being buffeted by the terrible storm, when it lurched this way and that, as it rose and fell again with frightening severity, when all the adults were scared half to death, that marvelous child was completely composed and unafraid." The minister could hardly believe his eyes.

It was not surprising therefore, that when the plane ultimately reached its destination and all the passengers were hurrying to disembark, our pastor lingered to speak with the girl whom he had watched for such a long time. Having commented about the storm and behavior of the plane, he asked why she had not been afraid. The sweet child replied, "Sir, my Dad is the pilot, and he is taking me home."

There are many kinds of storms that buffet us. Physical, mental, financial, domestic, and many other storms can easily and quickly darken our skies and throw our plane into apparently uncontrollable movement. We have all known such times, and let us be honest and confess, it is much easier to be at rest when our feet are on the ground than when we are being tossed about a darkened sky. Let us remember: Our Father is the pilot. He is in control and is taking us home. Don't worry.

Blessed Are They Whose Tower Leans

W hen I was a small child sitting at my desk in school, I was fascinated when the teacher told us about the Leaning Tower of Pisa. Probably this is why I always wanted to see it. When that day arrived, I stood enthralled before the structure that has charmed the whole world. The tower, which stands in Cathedral Square in Pisa, Italy, was commenced in A.D. 1170, but the building project had to cease for a time because it was discovered that the sandy soil could not support the weight. A few years later, it was considered safe to complete the eight stories of beautiful marble, and today, though leaning, the Tower attracts millions of visitors. The official guides have all kinds of stories to tell, but in essence they all say that one side of the Tower appears to rest on some kind of a fault in the earth, and in spite of repeated efforts by the authorities, the tower continues to sink. A few years ago, the Italian government poured hundreds of tons of cement into the foundations to arrest the leaning process, and now the tall building stays fourteen feet out of perpendicular. But a question remains. *If*—if the government *really* wished it to be upright, it could be dismantled piece by piece and erected on a solid foundation near at hand—but then it would no longer be attractive. From a financial point of view, it is better that the tower stays as it is. The authorities do not want it to fall, but neither do they wish it upright. It seems to be in their permissive will that for the benefit of all concerned, the tower should continue to lean.

I have been compelled to think about this. Have you ever felt that sinking feeling? Has your life ever seemed to be falling apart? Did you ever pray desperately that God would right what was so distressing and push you up straight again? Did your pride-and-joy tower of Pisa appear to be falling? Perhaps it never did fall, and never will fall, but on the other hand, it is not straight either. We are told that after wrestling with the angel, Jacob's thigh was out of joint (Gen. 32:24–28). Poor Jacob. God could have healed him, but he did not. With his thigh out of joint, Jacob became a better man than he ever was before. He became a great man of God. His leaning tower became very, very beautiful and famous. So, God knew what he was doing all the time. And so it is with us. Do not worry if your tower leans. The everlasting arms of God's love will never let it fall. Think about it, and keep on believing.

Blessed Are They Who Help an Enemy

O ne of my favorite authors is Norman Vincent Peale. I am one of millions of readers who have been thrilled by his stories about Americans. Not too long ago, I read one of his accounts about a drama in a courtroom. A Dr. McElhenney had fallen out with his medical partner, and the contention between them had become so sharp that the matter ended up in court. During the trial, Dr. McElhenney, who suffered from high blood pressure, suddenly lost consciousness and fell to the floor. He had experienced a form of heart seizure. He had no pulse and apparently had ceased breathing. Happily for him, the son of his former partner, the twenty-two year old Tim Hines was in the courtroom. This young man had once been a medical technician in the navy and he knew exactly what to do. He rushed to the fallen doctor, massaged his chest, and breathed life into him. Later, heart specialists said that Dr. McElhenney came as close to dying as a man can and still survive. Dr. Vincent Peale states that the lawsuit was dissolved from Dr. McElhenney's hospital bed and the entire matter was settled out of court. Later, the doctor, lifting his eyes toward heaven said, "There was a Judge in that courtroom, but he wasn't wearing robes."

Doubtless, Tim Hines responded instinctively without any thought of reward, but I cannot help but wonder if he had ever read the words of Paul, "Therefore, if thine enemy hunger, feed him; if he thirst, give him drink: for in so doing, thou shalt heap coals of fire on his head. Be not overcome of evil, but overcome evil with good" (Rom. 12:20–21). The world, with all its nations, is divided by many things. Not only does the sea separate us from each other but racial, political, cultural, and financial problems have shattered the peace of God's world. Yet, there are certain things beyond the bounds of language and culture that are understood instantly and are so powerful that all the differences can be swept aside.

No one needs to know the intricacies of grammar to understand and appreciate the warmth of a smile. It is not necessary to be a great scholar to recognize the charm of good music. But perhaps the greatest barrier-destroyer of all is kindness shown to an enemy. It is awfully difficult to be angry with someone who helps you; it is impossible to hate someone who persists in loving you. Perhaps this is the secret of the gospel and the reason why the church has grown throughout the ages. Real Christians love people, and that love has been expressed in innumerable ways. It conquered Saul of Tarsus, when outside the gates of Damascus he was determined to murder all the Christians he could find. It has challenged, charmed, and finally inspired many people whose one aim had been to destroy the faith of those who proclaimed the gospel of peace. Besides, being kind to others has a boomerang-like effect. What we give, returns; what we lose, multiplies. Do you have anyone in your little world who presents problems? Do you sometimes feel exasperated? What about loving that one person just a little bit more?

Blessed Are the Beautiful Dreamers

Sometimes our dreams never come true, but I guess much depends on what we dream and what we expect from life. Obviously, brides and grooms have their own conflicting ideas of future bliss, but true happiness only comes through giving and not through receiving.

I have just received from South Africa a marvelous photograph of a pet crow helping its owner weed the garden. The bird had been rescued when it was very young, and with care, the farmer had gently nursed it back to life. The baby had been starving to death. Soon that crow became like a member of the family. Day after day, the bird watched the man taking out weeds in his fields, and to the owner's delight, the crow now walks up and down the furrows, and with its long beak proceeds to pull out all the weeds it can find. It has learned never to touch the young plants. It also destroys the insects, and fights off all the other birds that try to steal the seedlings. It would seem that the bird is so filled with the spirit of thanksgiving that it now delights in helping the one who saved it. And, in giving of its love and service, at the same time it obtains its own food supply.

I am reminded again of the great Indian mystic Sadhu Sundar Singh who was traveling with two companions in the mountainous regions of northern India when a terrible storm swept down on them. Progress became most difficult and their lives were in danger. When one man collapsed, the other urged the Sadhu to leave him in the snow. The holy man refused to abandon the traveler, and in disgust and disdain, the other man pressed on alone. The Sadhu's act seemed suicidal, but lifting the fallen companion to his own shoulder, the Sadhu struggled to carry him through the storm. It was this added effort that kept the blood flowing in his own veins. As Sadhu Sundar Singh struggled over the mountain, he came to the place where the man who had left had fallen in the snow and was already dead. As St. Francis of Assisi rightly said, "It is in giving that we receive."

We are all dreamers—and it is nice to dream. As we live, let us all think of what we might do for others. How best can we show our gratitude to the people who have been good to us? A word of thanks, a warm handshake, a gift, or even just a smile might be a sunbeam sent down from heaven.

Blessed Are They Who Never Stop Looking

We are traveling along the great highway called "life," and as we enter the new year we shall pass another milestone. What do we expect to find in the next twelve months? In Hebrews 11:8–10, we read, "By faith, Abraham, when he was called to go out into a place which he should after receive for an inheritance, obeyed; and he went out, not knowing whither he went. . . . For he looked for a city which hath foundations, whose builder and maker is God." When this man answered God's call, he had to leave his home and begin a new life at the age of seventy-five. He did not know where he was going, but he trusted the strong hand of God to guide him. After he arrived in the Promised Land, Abraham still had to live in tents; the only land he ever owned was a burial plot that he purchased from a local inhabitant.

Yet, he was not disillusioned. Why was he content to live the life of a nomad even when he had become wealthy? He could have erected a walled city. He could have become a king and established a great kingdom. Abraham could have surrounded himself with all the comfort and security imaginable. Why did he not do so? "He looked for a city." Yes, his eyes were focused on a dwelling place far more secure and attractive. He was looking for a city whose designer and builder was God. He reminds me of John Bunyan who wrote *Pilgrim's Progress*. He, too, looked for a city—the Celestial City—that glorious place that awaited him at the end of the road.

When a person builds upon any self-made foundation, he does so only for a time. When one builds on the solid rock— Christ—one builds for eternity. W. Heartsell Wilson wrote:

> This is the beginning of a new day. God has given me this day to use as I will. I can waste it or use it for good. What I do today is important because I am exchanging a day of my life for it. When tomorrow comes, this day will be gone forever, leaving in its place something I have traded for it. I want it to be gain, not loss; good, not evil; success, not failure. Then I shall not regret the price I paid for it.

Yes, day after day, week after week, year after year, Abraham looked for a city, and thank God, in the end he found it. What shall we find this year? Nothing, unless we keep looking. Each and every day might introduce us to entrancing vistas of spiritual loveliness, and just beyond our present horizons, that city might be waiting. Don't let anything spoil your vision.

Blessed Is the Mother Who Is Truly Appreciated

During the summer of 1965, my husband and I stayed a week in the strange mystical land of India, and we shall never forget the experience. India is a land of wealth and poverty, of education and superstition. Ornate temples overshadow the wretchedness of many villages, and to hungry Indians, every American tourist must appear to be some kind of millionaire. We heard many tales and wondered at the legends believed by the village people.

The story is told of a beautiful Hindu princess who was appalled by the famine devastating the countryside. No rain had fallen, the crops had failed, and children were starving to death. The great lady sought the counsel of her wise advisors and they told her the only remedy would be a sacrifice to the gods. Some worthy person would have to die. After much thought, the princess decided that she could hardly ask another to sacrifice a life when she was the most worthy of all. She therefore issued the order that her burial place should be prepared. She would die for her people. Regretfully, her servants went to work, but as they were digging, they disturbed a spring of water which suddenly gushed from the earth. The legend states that the flow of water gathered intensity with every passing moment, until a beautiful river brought life and fertility to the land. The dark, lovely eyes of the Indian women flash with pride when they recount the story of their wonderful princess.

In some senses every mother is a princess. Every day as she sees to the needs of her family, she sacrifices, and from her inner-most resources, in strange and sometimes apparently magical ways, nourishment, cheer, encouragement, and help flow like a river to those around her. Alas, some mothers are not as appreciated as they should be. Gratitude, appreciation, thanks —sometimes these qualities seem to have disappeared from daily living. I have a neighbor who has just undergone serious surgery. When she returned from the hospital her grown son was a little irritated that she asked him to do certain chores. Finally, that lovely mother invited the son to see her wounds—her incision. He was shocked by what he saw, and then she explained, "Now you know why I asked you to do things for me." Not all women have the privilege of giving birth to a child, but happy are they who do. Happier still are the mothers who see appreciation shining in the eyes of their loved ones. Say "Thank you" to those who labor and care for you every day. It does not cost much to say those words, but they mean a great deal to the princess in your life. Without her aid, your world would be filled with drought; your life might be empty.

Blessed Are They Who Are Not a Disappointment to the Lord

A few days ago, I read in the magazine *The Prairie Overcomer* the most thought-provoking poem:

CHRIST'S PLAN FOR ME
When I stand at the judgment seat of Christ
And He shows me His plan for me,
The plan of my life as it might have been
Had He had His way, and I see—
How I blocked Him here, and I checked Him there
And I would not yield my will.
Will there be grief in my Savior's eyes—
Grief, though He loves me still?
He would have me rich, and I stand there poor
Stripped of all but His grace
While memory runs like a hunted thing
Down the paths that I cannot retrace.

Then my desolate heart will well nigh break
With tears that I cannot shed;
I shall cover my face with my empty hands;
I shall bow my uncrowned head.
Lord, of the years that are left to me
I give them to Thy hand.
Take me and break me, mold me now
To the pattern Thou hast planned.
                    —Martha Snell Nicholson

Not too long ago, I looked into the eyes of one of my dearest friends. I have known her for several years and I have grown to love her very much. A member of her family had grieved her beyond words, and no human effort could hide her disappointment. Yet, through her tear-filled eyes, a mother's love was still shining. Nothing on earth could destroy her love for a wayward son, but at that moment, it seemed nothing could ever take away her disappointment. As I think of her now, I am sure my heavenly Father could sympathize with that kind of woman. Surely, he has had much practice. God has loved his children with an everlasting love, but oh, how we disappoint him. We permit all kinds of little things to steal into our hearts and often, to remain there. But anything that displeases the Lord cannot be good for the health of his children. The other day, I came across a strange little note, that, the writer said, had addressed "her ever-present temptation." It read thus:

I have tried to love you lightly, but without success—
To love you very little, and never to excess.
I have sought to love you wisely—but this I
    cannot do,
For all my vows are shattered—each time I look
    at you.

So very often in these years, I have listened as pastors preached about the nearness of the Lord's return. Now, as I reflect on the messages, I remember one important text. It is found in 1 John 2:28. "And now, little children, abide in him; that, when he shall appear, we may have confidence, *and not be ashamed before him at his coming*" (emphasis added). Doubtless, he has a plan for all of us, and if we are faithful, he will reward us with a crown.

Blessed Are
the Praise Makers

Y ou will probably agree with me when I say that the late
Mr. Jimmy Durante was one of the best beloved of all the
American comedians. His tilted hat, sparkling wit, and above
all his oversized and unmistakable nose, which he affection-
ately called "snozzle," were his trademarks. There were many
great and memorable moments in his long life, but of them
all, one is specially remembered. It happened shortly after
World War II. One day he received a call from Ed Sullivan
who wanted Durante to go with him to a veterans' hospital to
entertain the many wounded and disabled veterans who were
receiving treatment. Durante told him that he would love to,
but that prior commitments made acceptance impossible. He
had two very remunerative radio shows to do on that date.
Sullivan assured him that these presented no problem. It
would be possible to go to the hospital early, do the show, and
have plenty of time to drive back to do the radio shows. Durante finally agreed but told Sullivan that he would only have
time for one number.

They drove out the following Sunday, and Durante went
through one of his routines. The audience was ecstatic and
pleaded for more. What happened then completely surprised

Sullivan who was watching from the wings. Durante accepted the applause, then grabbed the microphone and proceeded to do two more complete routines.

When he finally made his exit to a standing ovation from the vets, Sullivan said, "Jimmy, you were just great, but now you will never make your radio shows."

Jimmy replied, "Look at the front row of the audience and you will see why I forgot all about those dates." Sullivan poked his head through the curtains and saw two soldiers in the center of the front row. Each had lost an arm and were applauding by clapping their two remaining hands together.

Blessed indeed are the Praise Makers. The two men might have been glum and bitter because of their misfortune. Instead, they were enthusiastic, and helping each other, making it known to everybody that they could still laugh. Have you ever noticed how infectious laughter is? Have you ever walked through a room in which people were laughing? Surely, you paused to ask what was going on. Laughter is far more pleasant than a growl; a smile is more attractive than a scowl. Praise is a beautiful thing. It is a warm breeze on a cold day. It is a ray of sunshine when skies are overcast. Praise is the heart of true worship. When we concentrate our thoughts on thanking the One who has done so much for us, somehow we forget our losses and begin to count our gains. I may only have one arm, so to speak, but when I join with some other person who has similarly suffered, and when together we pool our resources to tell our benefactor how much we love him, then in a most wonderful way, our darkened skies begin to brighten. Let us make today—let us make every day—a day for praising God. Durante loved his applause from the two men—our Lord also loves to be thanked.

Blessed Are the Stupid

Ever since the days when my husband and I worked with the South African Baptist Church, I have been interested in ostriches. We were driving one day through Cape Province when we saw these strange ungainly birds strutting across the plains. They appeared awkward and a little stupid, for when they started to run, they spread wide their wings as if they were airplanes lowering their flaps. When I heard hunters telling stories of the way these birds, when frightened, buried their heads in the sand, it was easy to conclude that the ostriches were the fools in God's creation. Then, quite recently, my entire concept of these flightless birds changed.

Mr. Ari Cohen, our Israeli guide on a tour of Israel, recounted an experience he had had with an earlier group. In the course of his daily comments, he referred to the stupidity of the ostrich—and how it tried to hide from danger by burying its head in sand. One of the listeners was an ostrich farmer from South Africa who immediately contradicted what Ari had said. Obviously, he was well informed because he went on to describe how the female birds lay their three pound eggs in a single, large depression in the sand. Each egg has a capacity of about one and a half quarts. To guard the eggs, the male sits on them at night and the female takes her turn during the daytime. Often, when the bird seems to be burying its head, it is merely turning the eggs in the nest. He said the bird was fearless and one blow from its foot could rip open a man's face. Apparently, the bird lowers its head—not because of fear, but because this is the way in which it can watch the approach of its enemy. Looking between its feet, the ostrich knows when the foe is within reach, and suddenly, lashing out with its foot, the bird quickly destroys anyone who is threatening the nest. That tremendous bird cannot fly—but can it kick. The foolish things of this world are sometimes among the wisest.

I remember reading how Paul, in the first chapter of 1 Corinthians, wrote of the apparent foolishness of the Christians. When the saints "buried their heads" and refused to see the glamorous, glittering things of the world, the onlookers considered them to be mad. Yes, it is written, "God chose the foolish things of this world to confound the wise." As I look back and remember the things we have witnessed in our travels around the world, I appreciate to the full what Paul described. I have seen people making great sacrifices to help the cause of Christ. I have known people to suffer great humiliation rather than to hit back at enemies. I have heard the laughter and sneers of folk who did not understand the motives of the people who loved the Lord. But, as the years passed by, I watched those "fools for Christ," and *always,* in the end, they triumphed. They were not stupid—they were wise, and God blessed them. He always does.

Blessed Are They Who Are Able to Stand Against Pressure

During recent weeks, our yard, garden, and sidewalk have all been one big mess. I am sure that my spouse is more expert at handling texts than he ever will be handling bricks and cement. Alas, one of the retaining walls protecting our property had been slowly bulging during the passing of the years, and it had become obvious that something would have to be done to correct the fault. After every rainstorm, the large bank behind the wall would become sodden and the increasing weight threatened to push the wall over. My husband is not a builder, but he will have a go at anything. One morning, he started to take the wall down stone by stone and soon his muttering could be heard from Dan to Beersheba. He discovered that the wall was hollow. The former owner had built an ornamental, not a retaining, wall. All the cement bricks or blocks had empty interiors. The manufacturers had made them so that steel reinforcing rods could be passed throughout the wall, but the man who built ours apparently was short of both brains and cement. He forgot to put drainage holes at the bottom of the wall and left every block completely hollow. When the pressure behind the wall began to increase, something had to give.

As I have more or less suggested, my husband's comments were not very complimentary. Slowly, he dug back into the bank. I watched as, with patience, he filled the heart of every cement block before he replaced it, and I have to admit, the wall is now better and stronger than the original one.

And then, suddenly, I felt that the Lord was speaking to me. Pressure behind a retaining wall can be very dangerous, but there are many other kinds of pressure even more dangerous. When these begin to increase, many people feel overwhelmed. Unfortunately, some very tired souls, unable to cope, decide to end it all. Hollow bricks and hollow hearts seem to be cousins. Without that inner reinforcement that comes from God, I doubt if anyone could effectively withstand the enormous weight that threatens to break down our resistance. If the man who built our wall had taken time to pack every cement block, he would have prevented a lot of trouble. And if we take the time, especially in the mornings, to strengthen our souls with the Bread of Life and the richest kind of communion, we shall not crack and go to pieces during the day. Someone has said: "If you are too busy to pray, then you are too busy." I have often found that when I really get excited about some new treasure I have found in the Bible, I continue to think about it as I do my housework, and somehow, the frustrations, the strain, the little things that get under my skin seem to diminish. Every time I see my new wall, I shall remember that I, too, must develop more and more of that inner strength. Did Paul have this in mind when he wrote Ephesians 6:10–11? Somehow I think he did.

Blessed Are the Promises of God

My husband and I have been studying the Minor Prophets. I must admit I started the ball rolling. Some time ago, I became aware that I knew hardly anything about the section of the Bible that reaches from Hosea to Malachi. This worried me a little, and so one day I asked my husband if he would help me, and others, by producing something to explain more of this little-understood part of the Bible.

In my own private devotions, I have been reading the works of these prophets and certain verses have brought great blessing to my soul. For example, I have been thrilled by the striking contrast between two verses. Joel 1:4 tells of the great devastation that had come to Israel. "That which the palmerworm hath left hath the locust eaten; and that which the locust hath left hath the cankerworm eaten; and that which the cankerworm hath left hath the caterpillar eaten." The land of Israel was really in a mess. Yet, in Joel 2:25, we have the words, "And I will restore to you the years that the locust hath eaten." I would like you to notice how the word *years* is spelled. It is not ears, such as ears of corn, but years as in years of time that have been wasted. The end of a year is for both looking back and looking ahead. Few, if any of us, can look back without regrets. The locusts of one kind or another have surely invaded our "land," leaving their evil trademarks behind them. What might have been very fruitful crops within the soul somehow became spoiled, and we had to be content with second- and even third-rate results. Our harvest has been a very poor one. All of us could have done better. But it is refreshing to notice that the ancient prophet suddenly switched from ears to years. What Joel saw in the fields around him, he used as an illustration of greater things. Israel had been made aware of the devastation on the farms. God thought more of the barrenness within souls. But the spoiling effect of the locusts was not the final word. The promise of God was that he would restore what had been lost, and this applied not only to material blessing, but also to the spiritual. The Lord would make the desert to blossom as the rose. The memory of a poor season should never paralyze the arms of the farmer. If at first you don't succeed, try, try again. With that thought in mind, let us face the future boldly. Jesus *never* fails. Let us plant our fields again, for God is with us.

Blessed Are They Who Influence Others for Good

When in Australia, I was fascinated by a gap in the mountains—a gap through which the main highway ran. It had been discovered by an explorer called Cunningham who became famous for many things. He had strange habits, one of which was the filling of his coat pockets with seeds of all kinds. Today, in the most unlikely places, a traveler finds lemon and other fruit trees; the testimony to the seed sowing of that great pioneer in Australia. We all leave influences behind of one kind or another, and it behooves us to leave good ones.

A teacher left her class one day, and on returning, found the children sitting in profound silence with their arms folded. She was surprised by the silence in the classroom and asked for an explanation. A small girl arose to say, "Teacher, you told us one day that if you ever left the classroom and came back and found us all sitting perfectly silent, you would drop dead." I do not suppose for one moment that the teacher kept her promise, but at least she had some idea of the influence she was having on her students.

A very nice young lady was visiting recently, and when discussing certain people and their kindness to her she said, "It's nice to be loved." Probably the Lord had this in mind when he said, "And as ye would that men should do to you, do ye also to them likewise" (Luke 6:31). We can hardly expect to be loved if we scatter enmity. Oftentimes, others only reflect what we are. People are like mirrors—they give back only what they receive from us. If sometimes we do not like what we receive, we should consider well what we have given. To neglect doing good is to ask for trouble.

Recently in our home, we have been thinking about the Minor Prophets. It has been interesting to discover that when the archaeologists were digging in the ruins of Nineveh, they came across a library of clay tablets—the books of ancient times. Some of these contained the laws of the realm. One of the laws that operated in the ancient city said: If any man were guilty of neglect, he would be held responsible for the result of his neglect.

I cannot help but wonder what would be the effect upon America if such a law were in operation today. We hear so often about juvenile delinquency, but surely the ancients would have held the parents responsible for much of what the children do. What would the attitude of the Lord be toward his children who neglect to give the gospel to their neighbors or to send the message to people who live in darkness overseas? Will we be held responsible for the indifference that might cause eternal sorrow to those who have never heard of his grace and love? What influences are we leaving behind us?

Two small boys were walking home from the Sunday school where they had heard a lesson about the Devil. The one lad asked the other, "What do you think of this devil business?"

"Well," the other boy replied, "You know who Santa Claus turned out to be—it is either your father or your mother." Happy indeed are the parents who leave better and more lasting impressions on their family.

Blessed Are the Poles

One bright morning a few weeks ago, I walked out into my garden and there before me was a shadowy cross. For a moment or so it was truly startling. We have a telephone pole nearby, and the rising sun had cast its shadow across our lawn. As I looked around, I became aware of many other poles; in fact, Santa Barbara is filled with poles. Some carry telephone lines, others carry power lines, and still others carry the cables for television services. I have to admit that there is nothing attractive about poles, but life would lose many of its comforts without them. The telephone lines enable us to speak to and listen to our friends. They are our basic means of communication. The power lines bring us heat, light, and energy, and in winter without them, our homes would be refrigerators. Of course, we all know that by and through the cross of Calvary we are able to speak with God. We also know that what happened on that green hill became the means through which all the power of God can reach our hearts. But somehow, I cannot escape the conviction that we should be like poles throughout the kingdom of God. We may not be attractive, many of us are devoid of outstanding talents, but if somehow we can carry God's cables, our ministry might prove to be a vital part of God's planning.

Often, when I was a small child, I pulled out the petals on a daisy and counted as I went: "He loves me, he loves me not." To be loved is one of the greatest joys in life, but so many people do not know how much they are loved by the Lord. Maybe we could tell them. We might even become instrumental in starting up their own communication with God. Through us they might someday make contact with the Giver of every good and perfect gift. There is warmth in a genuine smile, there is cheer in the service expressed from a glowing heart. What flows through us might even light a fire in a heart that has been cold for years. If only we play our part, there is no end to what the Lord might be able to do. If only the Lord could express through us the music of the celestial city, much the strain and discord around us might vanish.

I liked the title to this chapter, "Blessed Are the Poles." But then another thought occurred to me—in order to become effective, those poles, or should I say, "those trees," had to die. They lost their life to serve humankind. They were cut down only to rise again. They were stripped of their natural beauty only to be given a privilege they had never known earlier. Did Paul have something of this in mind when he said, "I am crucified with Christ: nevertheless I live; yet not I, but Christ liveth in me" (Gal. 2:20)? We may not be able to sing, speak, or preach, but we can all be poles.

Blessed Are They Who Follow the Map

Some time ago, I listened as the wife of a local minister gave a minisermon to a group of children. The dear woman really blessed my soul. She, with her husband, had come from Kentucky to take charge of a church in Santa Barbara, and even her rich southern accent charmed me. During the previous week, her husband had been in the St. Francis Hospital for surgery, and, being a stranger in California, the wife did not know how to reach it. When she asked a friend for directions, she was told the way to go, but when she asked another friend, she was given a completely new set of directions. Seemingly everybody had a different way of getting to the same destination. The dear woman confessed that it was very confusing. My husband whispered to me, "The quickest way to St. Francis Hospital is to get hit by a truck."

The speaker explained that when they came all the way from Kentucky, they had no need to ask anybody which way to go. They had a map and faithfully followed its directions. Everybody in the church was fascinated when she went on to say that we are all on a journey—hopefully to heaven. Unfortunately, there are so many different voices offering directions that it has become easy to get lost. Some suggest we should join a church, or live exemplary lives. Others suggest the giving of donations to worthy causes. There are so many ideas that one wonders which is the right way to go. Then the speaker held up her Bible and told us how God had provided a map and that its directions are clear and plain. There is no need for anyone to get lost because the Lord Jesus said, "I am the way, the truth and the life: no man cometh unto the Father, but by me" (John 14:6). She explained that merely reading the map never got anybody anywhere. Unless the reading of the map is followed by faithful action, the reader has only wasted time. We must *obey* what the book says.

We can be washed from our sins by the power of the precious blood of Jesus. We can invite the Lord to live in our hearts, and, remembering his promise never to leave us, can enjoy the benefit of sharing fellowship with him as we journey along the highway of life. You see, Jesus knows the way to go, and no one ever got lost while staying close to the heavenly Guide. The woman went on to explain that Jesus never promised the way would be easy to travel. Other roads might seem more inviting; one very broad road offers all kinds of attractions, but alas, it only leads to destruction. The way to heaven sometimes might be steep and difficult, but if people really desire to go there, then they must follow the right and proper way as it is outlined in God's map—the Bible. Since many other people have already traveled the way safely, we can do so too, but the secret to getting to heaven is to stay close to Jesus. I was so blessed, for the children's story was indeed the gospel we love so much. Blessed indeed are they who follow the map. Avoid side roads, and you will get there.

Blessed Are They Who Know Where to Find the Spring

Today, plumbing has come to Nazareth, but years ago there was only one source of water for the whole of the town, and to that solitary spring even Joseph, Mary, and Jesus had to come for their supplies. In 1965, I went to see the simple archway under which the water ran. Some years afterward, I again visited Nazareth and was interested to see that a change had taken place. The simple archway of the past had been replaced by an elaborate, ornate arch on the other side of the busy street. We were told that because of the danger of accidents, the local authorities had decided to reroute the spring to make it surface where people could see and drink safely. Prior to our visit this year, I had told members of our party about this important link with the past, but when we arrived in Nazareth, I was somewhat dismayed to find there was no water whatsoever at the old archway. Surely, something had gone wrong. When we asked what had taken place, we were told a fascinating story. The spring had suddenly disappeared. This naturally worried the local inhabitants, for that famous source of water brought thousands of visitors to

Nazareth every year. Some enterprising citizen decided to seek the cause of the catastrophe, and so the workmen commenced digging. After quite a lot of work, they began to see that once again the soil was becoming moist and they knew they were on the right track. Then, quite suddenly they found the spring; as fresh and powerful as ever it had been—it had merely changed its course, and had pushed its way to the surface right beneath the altar in the nearby St. Gabriel's Church. This caused excitement among the congregation, and within a short time, a neat flight of steps was constructed so that sightseers could descend to see the rediscovered spring. Of course, this meant a revival of finances for the church, for whenever visitors come in, an official is at the door soliciting gifts for his cause.

To say the least, I was enthralled by this story. It seemed to suggest there are lives from which the living waters have vanished. Souls that once were fruitful gardens are now a wilderness. Men and women once so attractive and radiant are now morose and sad. The spring has disappeared. Happy indeed is the person who knows where to look for it. I think you will all know what I mean when I say that the best place to start looking is beneath the altar. I have often heard preachers speaking of how Abraham, who, having made a mess of his life in Egypt, decided one day that he would return "to the altar which he had made there at the first" (Gen. 13:3–4). There, the patriarch rediscovered the lost spring of fellowship; there, life started again. Do you ever feel dried up? Look for the spring near the Cross.

Blessed Are
the Godly Mothers

My mother has long since joined my father in heaven, but I remember so well the time when she was a young woman and I but a schoolgirl. Altogether, we were eight children—four boys and four girls, but as Kate Douglas Wiggin wrote: "Most of all the other beautiful things in life come by twos and threes; by dozens and hundreds. There are plenty of roses, stars, sunsets, rainbows, brothers and sisters, aunts, uncles, and cousins, but for us all, there is only one mother in all the world." Naturally, to me, mine was very special. Mary Allread Baker must have had a mother just like mine, for she wrote:

> She could not paint, nor write, nor rhyme
> Her footprints on the sands of time
> As some distinguished women do.
> Just simple things of life she knew—
> Like tucking little folks in bed,
> Or soothing someone's aching head.
> She was no singer, neither blessed
> With any special loveliness.
> To win applause and passing fame,

No headlines ever blazed her name.
But, oh, she was a shining light
To all her loved ones, day and night.
Her home—her kingdom, she its queen.
Her reign was faithful, honest, clean.
Impartial, loving, just to each
And every one she sought to teach.
Her Name? Of course, there is no other
In all the world so sweet—just Mother.

It has sometimes been said that a mother is the only one who can divide her love among many children, and at the same time give all her love to each and every one. My mother was a seamstress, and when the depression filled Wales with urgent need, she would sit for days and weeks at her sewing machine. She never had any ambition to become wealthy, but even when her fingers became sore, she would persevere in an effort to help my dad put bread on our table. I remember how she would make her family eat a meal while she was busy elsewhere. There was often insufficient food for everybody, so she would wait until everybody was filled. Sometimes there was nothing left for her. That was my mother.

She gave me and the rest of the family many things, but the greatest treasure ever bequeathed was her faith in the Savior, and her never-dying love for his cause. Mother never pestered me when I went out dancing all night; seldom scolded me without very great cause. She was gentle, kind, and thoughtful. I always knew she was praying for me, and the tears of joy that she shed when I became a Christian were precious. Blessed indeed is a godly mother—she is more to be desired than riches. If your mother is still here, be sure she knows that you love her.

Blessed Are They Who Soar with Eagles and Work with Turkeys

The other day, my husband officiated at the wedding ceremony of two of our best friends. After the ceremony, we stopped at a restaurant to get our lunch, and it was there that I suddenly saw a plaque on the wall. I have not been able to forget the startling words printed on it:

It is hard to soar with eagles when you have to work with turkeys!

I concluded that the person who wrote that message had two turkeys in his mind. Naturally, as the owner of a restaurant, he would have to handle real turkeys, but probably he was thinking of "human turkeys" too, who have the tendency to make one's days difficult. I admit, the more I think about that statement, the more I appreciate the sentiments. Turkeys spend their lives pecking, scratching, and gobbling. They seldom look up, for day after day their beaks are in the dust. It is certain that they *never* soar with eagles. The human species tends to clip the wings of those who would, if they could, "mount up with wings as eagles" (Isa. 40:31).

If Moses could have seen that plaque, I am sure he would have hung it over the entrance to his tent. Poor man, he spent much of his life trying to lead thousands of stupid turkeys toward the land of Canaan, and in the end, they pecked at him so persistently that he lost his opportunity for "soaring" in Canaan's skies. Let us admit candidly, it is hard to remain sweet when you are surrounded by people who are sour. It is hard to run with patience the race that is set before us, when all around are people who hold us back. It is almost impossible to spend time in the secret place when meals have to be prepared, dishes washed, clothes mended, shopping done, telephone calls answered, and washing, ironing, and cleaning seem to blot out the blue skies.

In one way or another, Moses knew most of these difficulties, but in spite of them he managed to soar with eagles. In fact, he soared so high that he really flew close to the Son of Righteousness, and as a result, the skin of his face started to shine. The Bible shares with us his tremendous secret—he went up the mountain to talk with God. He stayed there a whole day and then decided to stay another, and another, and another. Of course, we cannot do that, but at least we know his secret. To soar through heaven's skies unhindered, the eagle must have power within—power to carry it above the force of the earth's gravitational pull. We, too, must have a similar urge within our spirits, and the way to get it is by climbing the mountain. We may only be able to stay five or ten minutes, but the result makes the climb worthwhile. Then, when we work with turkeys, perhaps they too will notice that something has happened to us. They will see it is better to fly than to scratch in the soil. It is better to see a sunrise than to look for worms in dirt.

Blessed Are They Who Are Honest

Y ears ago, when my husband and I were working in
Australia, we met a most unusual man whose story we
have never forgotten. He lived in a small country town and
was known far and wide for the brand of tea that he sold. He
owned a grocery store and belonged to one of our churches.
He told us of a commercial artist who had visited him one
year. After completing his business, the man departed but,
unfortunately, forgot his valuable watch. The grocer found it
later, but had no idea where he could possibly find its owner.
One year later, the artist again walked into the store and was
delighted when the grocer produced the treasure that had long
since been given up as forever lost. When he offered a reward,
he was politely refused. The storekeeper explained that he was
a Christian and there was no need for any compensation
merely for his doing his duty. The artist thought for a moment and then came up with what we all now think was a
marvelous idea. Knowing the man to be well known as a tea
merchant, he drew a large capital T and then sketched a parrot sitting on it. When the grocer seemed a little puzzled by
the sketch presented to him, the artist explained what was on
his mind: On his tea, is the best poll I see.

It seems incredible now that the sketch and its message should have become a part of our language. That drawing was painted above the doorway of our friend's store, and at the time of our visit, it seemed to be the pride and joy of the Christian grocer. The saying: "Honesty is the best policy" is now known wherever the English language is spoken. A very small acorn has grown into a very great tree. I cannot help but think of yet another old saying: "Oh, what a tangled web we weave when first we practice to deceive." It pays to be honest—especially in our dealings with God.

We must be honest in our giving. God says in Malachi 3:10, "Bring ye all the tithes into the storehouse, that there may be meat in mine house, and prove me now herewith, saith the LORD of Hosts, if I will not open you the windows of heaven, and pour you out a blessing, that there shall not be room enough to receive it." Unfortunately, Ananias and Sapphira ignored this promise. They tried to deceive God and died for their folly (see Acts 5).

We must be honest in our loving. Sometimes an ounce of real love is worth a ton of money. To donate liberally and to love frugally is a tragedy. Mark 12:41–43 tells of a widow who cast all she had into God's treasury. It was true that she only gave two mites—but it represented all that she had. Of course, she could have kept one mite for herself—or could she have? Oh, how that woman must have loved God.

We must be honest in our trying. Paul said in Philippians 3:13–14, "forgetting those things which are behind, and reaching forth unto those things which are before, I *press* toward the mark" (emphasis added). Surely, we could do so much more for Christ if we really tried.

Blessed Are They Who Think of Others

The other day, in one of my books, I came across an old fable about a disgruntled old horse in his stall. With disdainful eye he had watched the stable hand carelessly spilling a handful of oats on the floor. The horse, muttering and moaning, said, "That clumsy fellow. He can't even put oats in my box without spilling them. I could have eaten that extra mouthful, but now it is wasted. If that fellow would only attend to his work, we would all be a lot happier in this place."

But as he thus soliloquized, a few pigeons flew in through the open door, settled on the floor, and happily started to pick up the grain. And as they ate, one wise bird said to the others, "I told you birds to trust the Lord and hunt, and he would send us our dinner." Then, when they had cleaned up all the grain in sight, a small mouse ran out and dug a dozen kernels out of the cracks where the pigeons had missed them. When she scurried off with her prize, the horse heard a tiny rustling noise, and bending down for a closer look, he saw a string of ants carefully gathering up the tiny specks of grain that were too small for anyone else to be bothered with. To the ants, each fragment was a capacity load. They could not have carried anything larger. When the ants had gone, according to the

fable, the old horse lifted his head toward heaven and apolo-
gized to the Creator for his critical spirit. Afterward he said, "I
guess the Lord knows the needs of every one of his creatures. I
will never again try to tell him how to run the world."

I think we can all find a place in our hearts for that old
horse. It is so easy to be critical of others, particularly if we are
not too pleased with what we see taking place around us. Paul
said, "And we know that all things work together for good to
them that love God, to them who are the called according to
his purpose" (Rom. 8:28). Probably every one of us has quoted
that text from time to time, but I wonder whether or not we
truly believe it. Basically, our job is to get on with the business
of loving God. His job is to make all the circumstances of life
work together for our good.

There have been occasions when I have been too concerned
with God's part of the bargain and not concerned enough with
my own. When I try to make all the details of life fit into some
sensible, understandable pattern, I only produce chaos. When
failure succeeds failure, we are apt to give up in disgust and
despondency. Sometimes I wonder if God ever shakes his head
in amazement when he sees how silly we are. If a handful of
oats seems out of place in our lives, we are sure that we are
heading straight for seven years of famine. Then we begin to
worry until peace is but a memory. Yet, even the blunder of
spilled oats can bring blessing to another.

Blessed Are They Who Make Time to Listen

Have you ever noticed that life seems to be one endless rush? The older one becomes, the shorter the days, the weeks, and the years seem. I am constantly hearing people ask: "Where has this year gone?" Breakfast is followed by lunch, and that is followed by dinner. Dishes have to be washed and clothes laundered. Meals have to be planned and prepared, shopping must be done, and always, without fail, on the busiest of busy days, some unexpected caller arrives to ruin half a day. It has often been said that the best made plans of mice and men will be spoiled, but it is extremely irritating when this happens to us. Blessed indeed is the person who remains calm in such moments; who listens to whispers, when other voices are demanding attention.

At one time, we had in our church a very fine man who was acting as the interim pastor. His name was the Rev. T. Arthur Smith, and in the course of a sermon, he related a simple story that I have never forgotten. Speaking of a former church in Kansas, he mentioned a small boy whose name was

Marion. That child became the pastor's shadow. Obviously, he was attracted to the minister, but unfortunately, he would arrive to ask questions at the most inopportune moments. Many busy mornings were absolutely ruined by the little fellow who would knock on the office door, and then enter to ask all kinds of questions. The preacher admitted that there were times when it was a little difficult to remain calm under the childish barrage of inquiries. Yet, somehow he always managed to do so. He would sit and chat with the little boy and became almost like another father to him—even though he desperately wanted to get on with his preparation for Sunday's sermon.

Then, as the pastor reminisced, and as we listened, he said quietly, "Had I known then what that lad was to become, I might have devoted more time to the child. Today, Marion is a full colonel in the United States Armed Forces; he is a chaplain and a teacher of other preachers." A strange, heart-warming stillness filled the church when the story ended.

Blessed indeed is the one who makes time to listen. I am wondering today if the Lord had similar thoughts in mind when he said, "Be still, and know that I am God" (Ps. 46:10). Paul, writing to his son in the faith, Timothy, said, "To Timothy, my dearly beloved son . . . I have remembrance of thee in my prayers night and day; greatly desiring to see thee. . . . From a child thou hast known the scriptures, which are able to make thee wise unto salvation through faith which is in Christ Jesus" (2 Tim. 1:2–3; 3:15). We know that Paul went to Timothy's hometown and was acquainted with Timothy's mother and grandmother. I cannot help but wonder if, in the early years, the young lad was also Paul's shadow. If so, I am sure that the great apostle made time to listen. Never despise an acorn—it might become a strong oak some day.

Blessed Are the Camel Christians

The camel at the close of day,
Kneels down upon the sandy plain;
To have his burden lifted off,
And rest to gain.
My soul, thou too shouldst to thy knees,
when daylight draweth to a close;
And let thy Master lift thy load
And grant repose.
Else, how canst thou tomorrow meet
With all tomorrow's work to do
If thou thy burden all the night
Dost carry through.
The camel kneels at break of day
To have the guide replace his load,
Then rises up again to take
The desert road.
So thou shouldst kneel at morning's dawn
That God may give thee daily care;
Assured that He no load too great,
Will make thee bear.

—Anna Temple

People have named camels the ships of the desert, and it seems to be a most fitting name. These animals are able to travel long distances across burning deserts, and probably without them, the Bedouins would not be able to exist. It has been claimed that a racing camel can travel one hundred miles in a single day. With their built-in water supply and with their great flat feet, these amazing creatures can speed along where all others would be bogged down. Our Lord often saw camels crossing the paths ahead, and it is not surprising that some of his most powerful illustrations mention them. All this I have known for a long, long time, but the poem with which I began this message seems to have added importance to it today.

For many people, life is indeed a desert, and every day a hazardous experience into the unknown. So often, one begins the day in the midst of green pastures and beside still waters, and then suddenly the scenery changes. The entrancing beauties quickly disappear; the springs of living water dry up, and before we know what has happened, we feel that progress is impossible. I have known days like this, and so have you. That is just the reason why we need to look again at our old friend, the camel. If he can succeed in his strange world, then perhaps we can succeed in ours. We must begin aright; we must finish aright. In the morning, we kneel to receive grace and strength to carry the load; in the evening, we kneel in gratitude, hopefully to lose our load for a while and to rest.

Have you ever stayed awake for hours worrying about this and that? Have you tossed and turned in bed? It really is an awful experience, for in the early hours of the morning, every molehill of difficulty becomes a mountain of impossibility. Yes, I have known such experiences and that is why I am willing for an old camel to teach me. I know I belong to the One who will never overload me.

Blessed Are They Who Have Seen the Beauty of Jesus

During our worldwide travels for Christ, my husband and I met many wonderful people. Among them were Dr. and Mrs. Philip Ray, whom we first met in South Africa. At that time, they were in charge of a church in Grahamstown. Since then, they have held pastorates in America, but when nearing the age of retirement, instead of resting, these great servants of God returned to South Africa once again to help extend the kingdom of Christ in that needy country. Throughout the years, they have kept in touch with us, and I received a wonderful letter from them relating the following event:

A missionary friend from the Transkei went to seek out one of his students recently. The student is now a black African evangelist living completely by faith. After days and days of searching, the missionary discovered where his former student lived and arrived to find a grain tank turned upside down with a hole cut out for a doorway. The young wife, with two small children greeted him. The godly evangelist had been ill for two weeks with a fever, and was under a sack on the bare floor. The missionary called out, and the black evangelist simply looked up and said, "Isn't Jesus wonderful?" Lying there in the dust, ill and destitute, Jesus remained everything to him. The missionary had found him, and he knew that help would soon be forthcoming.

Yes, Jesus is certainly wonderful. Long ago, the prophet Isaiah said, "For unto us a child is born, unto us a son is given: and the government shall be upon his shoulder: and his name shall be called Wonderful" (Isa. 9:6). The Lord Jesus is marvelous in so many different ways that it is very difficult to express all that we feel about him.

I read the other night how a small girl, looking at a tall pine tree, asked a forest ranger, "Why do people call this tree 'the lodgepole pine?'" The ranger replied, "Do you see how tall and straight this kind of tree grows? That is the answer. The Indians discovered it to be just what they needed for their tepee poles."

"Do you know," he continued, "there is another interesting thing about this tree. See upon the very tip-top how its cones are all clustered? These cones never open up unless there is a very severe forest fire. That is how woody plants are replaced after the forest has been destroyed by fire. Beneath the ashes of destruction, the seeds are sheltered. After a while, they reproduce the forest. So from the ashes of destruction comes life." How true this was of the One whose birth we celebrate. From the divine seed planted in a virgin's womb, he grew to be the tallest, best, and straightest of all God's creation. Then came the fires of destruction that apparently ended his life. But he rose again, and, because of his death, millions have found a new life. Oh yes. "Isn't Jesus wonderful?"

Blessed Are They Who Turn Mistakes into Stepping-stones

The only way to offset the darkness of an approaching cloud is to look for its silver lining. And of equal importance, the *only* way to deal with unpleasant failures is to find a way to turn defeat into victory. Surely, the Lord knew this when he warned Peter of the soon-to-be disaster when Peter would deny his Lord. The disciple also knew it when he looked back and remembered how he had failed. Sometimes an error can lead to unprecedented success.

Today, we seldom, if ever, use blotting paper, but there was a time when everyone wrote with pen and ink. At first, the only way to dry the ink quickly was to "pepper" it with sand. Yet, a sand box was a clumsy way of making sure a letter was not smeared. One day, a woman in a Berkshire paper mill forgot to add size to a run of paper. It was a great mistake, and many yards were completely wasted. A member of the firm happened to use a fragment of the discarded paper to write a note. He found that what he had written became almost immediately illegible. Then he discovered that the "spoiled" paper was a perfect medium for drying ink by absorbing it. That was how blotting paper came into being. It reminds us that it is not a good thing to make mistakes, but if we do, we can sometimes profit by them.

After the crucifixion, some unwise people might have questioned the wisdom of God. Did he not permit his Son to become the victim of a Jewish mob? Everything appeared to have been ruined when the Man of Galilee was taken to a cross and crucified. But was it a mistake? No. God turned what seemed to be a disaster into an overwhelming triumph, for now he had a way to blot out our transgressions. The Lord now had the means by which he could turn his enemies into friends.

I love the story that tells of Abraham Lincoln's attitude toward his foes during the Civil War. He was always unwilling to be hard on his enemies, and one day a woman asked why this was so. Lincoln, in characteristic manner replied, "What, madam? Do I destroy them when I make them my friends?"

We all make many mistakes, but God can help us overcome them. With his help we can turn them into stepping-stones. Then, in his sight, we shall be found acceptable. The author Francis Gray was walking along a river bank one day when he came upon an old fisherman. They talked together and then the old man produced a card and asked, "Have you seen this?" It read:

> God grant that I may live to fish
> Until my dying day.
> And when it comes to my last cast,
> I'll then most humbly pray.
> When in the Lord's safe landing net,
> I'm peacefully asleep,
> That in His mercy I'll be judged
> *As good enough to keep!*

My old dad in Wales was a fisherman. I think he and many others would like *The Fisherman's Prayer.*

Blessed Are the Patient

In her delightful book, *Lord of the Valleys*, Florence Bulle tells a delightful story about Dr. Phillips Brooks. She described how the great man was pacing his study like a caged lion, but when he was asked the cause of his concern, he replied, "The trouble? I'm in a hurry and God isn't. That's the trouble." From time to time, every Christian on earth has been aware of the same kind of problem. We have all asked, "Why does God not do something? He is so slow." Sometimes the Lord's seeming inactivity has propelled us into our own actions and then, very painfully, we have learned how "fools rush in where angels fear to tread."

Some years ago, I read about a small piece of ebony that complained when its owner whittled away, filling it with rifts and holes. The carver, however, paid no attention to the complaints. He was making a flute and was too wise to discontinue his efforts each time the wood complained. Yet, his kindly face seemed to say, "Little friend, without these rifts and holes and the painful cutting, you would only be a black stick—just a piece of ebony of no use whatever. What I am doing now may seem heartless. It may appear as if I am destroying you, but no, I know what I am doing. I am changing you into a flute whose music will charm and comfort many sorrowing hearts. My shaping is the making of you, for only thus will you be able to fulfill my plans."

How easy it would be to appreciate the complaint of the piece of ebony. Have we not all asked at one time or another: "Will he never stop hurting me?" A building being cleaned by the sandblasting process might ask the same question. The blunt chisel on a grinding wheel might also do so. A piece of steel in the blacksmith's fire might complain, as would a suffering body beneath the probing knife of a kindly surgeon. The little word, *why*, has been used perhaps more than any other word in the dictionary, and so often there appears to be no response. Yes, our heavenly Father seems to be very slow.

I was fascinated when I read how the Dutch people cultivate new varieties of roses. They plant a mediocre bush close to a lovely bloom of superior quality and then watch the inferior plant very carefully. When the anthers on the stamens develop, they remove them to prevent any form of pollination. The object of placing the inferior rose bush so close to the beautiful variety is to have the golden dust from the stamens of the valuable roses fall upon the deprived buds of the other. I believe that in all this there is a parable for us. Sometimes the so-called cruel hand of the gardener keeps on taking from us what we consider to be a most essential part of our existence. The question hammers away at our minds like a battering ram: "Why does he do this to me?" Maybe heaven's Gardener wants some of the precious golden dust of the glory land to fall on our poor inferior souls so that under his watchful eye, we, too, might develop the loveliness that is so characteristic of all who live close to the Savior. Even if God seems slow, he is always thoughtful. Remember that.

Blessed Are They Who Pull Together

Each day is a link between the past and the future, and I am never more conscious of this than I am at Christmas and New Year. My thoughts often go back to the time when my mother was the joy of our home. Rummaging among my treasures, I found an old autograph album dating back to the days of my childhood, and there in her shaky handwriting was a message:

> And when the One Great Scorer
> Comes to write against your name,
> He marks not that you won or lost,
> But how you played the game.

Let me confess candidly that I am not a football fan, but recently I read the testimony of "Tex" Coulter, a rugged 260–pound football tackle from Fort Worth, Texas. He won all-American honors two years in succession while playing for the great Army teams of 1944 and 1945. He wrote:

It's easy to be selfish and vain on the football field. You can read too many clippings
about yourself, or let the roar of the crowd go to
your head. Sometimes I felt a special urge to show
what a powerhouse of action I could be—a rock
on defense, a dynamo on offense. It's human to
have such temptations, but to let them run away
with you?—that's bad. A football eleven can have
eleven All-Americans, one for every position, but
if each is trying to be a star on his own, any well-
trained team with moderately good players can
beat the daylights out of it.

Mr. Coulder goes on,

The game of football helps me to realize that
life is also a game, with God keeping account
of every yard gained or lost. I like to think now
that I am playing on his team.

Yes, I suppose it is quite natural that we all want to be stars
in our own right, but so often true victory and lasting happiness only come when we forget personal glory, and contribute
more to the success of the team. Sometimes even the work of
the church is hindered by people who wish to operate in the
limelight. I have known elderly people who resented any
younger worker taking a long cherished position on this or that
committee. Yes, it takes grace to stand aside for another to take
one's place—but it takes all the grace and glory of God for the
one who stepped aside to help make his successor an even
greater triumph within the church.

But is not that what Christianity is all about? We work together with the Lord, and recognizing that others share our
desire to glorify Christ, we learn to live and sacrifice as a team.
It is true that at the end of a football season the records might
show that a certain player scored a certain number of

touchdowns, but every wise coach also knows that those touchdowns were made possible by other unselfish men who contributed to the all-around effort. If God is the coach of our team, then let us do our utmost in every detail and phase of life's game. If we live and work to please him, as the players say, "We shall never be discharged."

Blessed and Wise Are the Compassionate

Mr. Fiorello La Guardia, one of the most famous mayors of New York City, used to be a judge at a police court. One day, the police brought before him a trembling old man who was charged with stealing a loaf of bread. The old man said he had to do it because his family was starving. "Well, I have to punish you," said Mr. La Guardia. "The law makes no exception, and I can do nothing except sentence you to a fine of ten dollars." Then he added, after reaching into his pocket, "And here are the ten dollars to pay your fine. Furthermore," he said as he threw another dollar into the man's hat, "I am going to fine everyone in the courtroom fifty cents for living in a town where a man has to steal bread in order to eat." So he passed the hat around, and the old man, with the light of heaven in his eyes, left the courtroom with $47.50.

A person's face can be a window through which people may look into the soul. It may scowl and reveal bitterness. It may smile and reveal tenderness. The modern saying: "What you see is what you get," can be very true in so many ways. Blessed indeed are the compassionate; blessed are they whose eyes reflect the love of Christ.

When Adoniram Judson went as a missionary to Burma, he was treated cruelly by the people. He was put into a filthy prison to be tortured day and night. He was chained and suffered beyond measure. When, after many terrible years in Burma, he returned to America, a small boy watched him coming off the ship and recognized him from a picture he had seen in a newspaper. The lad ran up the street to tell his pastor, and the minister hurriedly went with the boy to the dockside. Yes, the lad was right. This was indeed Adoniram Judson. The pastor and the missionary talked for a long time and forgot all about the youngster who had made the meeting possible. But the lad stood there silent and eager, unable to tear himself away from the wonderful sight of the missionary's face. Even after all that Mr. Judson had suffered, peace, love, and joy shone from his countenance.

Many years later, that same boy, Henry Clay Trumbull, became a famous minister himself and ultimately became the editor of *The Sunday School Times*. He wrote a book in which there was a chapter entitled, "What a Boy Saw in the Face of Adoniram Judson." Much time had passed since the homecoming of the famous missionary, but the lad had never been able to forget the tenderness that shone from the saint's eyes. Judson obviously knew what the Lord meant when he said, "Blessed are ye, when men shall revile you, and persecute you and shall say all manner of evil against you falsely, for my sake. Rejoice, and be exceeding glad: for great is your reward in heaven" (Matt.5:11–12). Today, unfortunately, families, communities, churches and even nations exhibit bitterness. Let us resolve that each day we shall be numbered among the compassionate and be wise indeed.

Blessed Are They Who Stand at God's Right Hand

Years ago, my husband was preaching in Woodland Hills, California. I went with him for the day, and I am so glad that I did. I shall never forget what happened that Sunday morning. On the Saturday before, terrible fires had devastated the district, and homes had been destroyed. I had watched the telecasts from the area and had been dismayed by the heartrending scenes. Then suddenly, one man was brought before the cameras, and what he said thrilled my soul. He told how the men in charge had advised his family to stay indoors, but he went on to say, "My wife and children were in there praying, when suddenly, the Lord told us to get out fast. This we did, but only just in time, for as we left, the entire house burst into flames." I did not know when I watched that man on television that I was to meet him the next morning.

As we drove to the church, we saw the hills still smoldering and a huge mass of smoke hung over the entire district. Eventually we found the church where the first service was to begin at 8:30 A.M. The pastor stood in the pulpit and expressed sympathy for one of the members who had lost everything except the clothing he and his family were wearing. He said, "This brother and his family are here with us. Perhaps he would like to give a testimony."

As I watched, the young man I had seen on television stood and said, "Thank God, we are here." He was holding his Bible, the only thing saved from the fires. Quietly, he continued, "All the material things have gone, but the real treasures still remain," and he looked at his wife and three small sons. I could have wept.

A Scripture came alive for us all that morning. The pastor drew attention to the church bulletin where we read that Psalm 16 was the meditative Scripture for the day. Anyone was welcome to express a thought concerning it. No one responded until my husband, who had been deep in thought, rose to stand beside the minister. He asked us to read carefully verses 8 and 11. He indicated that in verse 8, David spoke of his own right hand—"because he is at my right hand, I shall not be moved." Then in verse 11 David spoke of God's right hand—"at thy right hand there are pleasures for evermore." Then my husband did something I had never seen him do before. As he stood alongside the pastor, he said, "You see, the pastor is at my right hand—there he is." But then he paused and asked, "Brother, where is your right hand?" When the minister raised his right hand (on the other side of his body), my husband said, "Oh, but that is a long way off—it is away over there." Then pausing to let this sink into our minds, he finally added: "It is impossible for the pastor to stand at my right hand, and for me to stand at his right hand—unless I turn him around so that *we are facing each other*." It was all so simple and yet so effective.

The congregation was hushed, and the man who had been delivered from the fires sat as one entranced. His eyes were stars. He understood.

Blessed Are
the Dedicated Young

Have you ever wanted to be young again? Have you ever looked into the mirror to see unwanted wrinkles beginning to appear, and the strands of grey hair beginning to show? The aging process is something most people would like to stop. There have been occasions when I wished I could become a young woman again, but for the most part, I am exceedingly happy with what God has allowed me to see and do. Yet, I must admit that on Sunday evening when I saw a film being shown by a representative of the Wycliffe Translators the urge to become young again was very strong within my soul. The young lady, a missionary home on furlough, told us about her work in New Guinea and the longer she talked, the more deeply stirred I became. Afterward, my husband confessed that he, too, had felt the same way.

She explained to the audience that in Papua, New Guinea, the center of life, the emotions, happiness, and so forth, is not the heart. For example, when one of the old men had sat enjoying a marvelous meal, he had said, "Oh, my throat is so happy." She told us that when the people were invited to accept Christ as their Savior, they were encouraged to "let him come into your throat."

We were all fascinated as she described how, while living in New Guinea, they had to search intensely for every word, and sometimes found it extremely difficult to get a word to explain a Bible truth. For example, they could not find a word for forgiveness. Then one day, when they were dedicating a new building, the people came to join hands and form a circle around the structure. They were all singing and having a good time, when quite spontaneously, the people let go of each others' hands and instead placed them around each others' shoulders. The missionary had never seen this happen before, so she asked one of the men what was taking place. He explained that this was something very special. He used a word she had never heard and told her that this only happened when they told each other they were going to forget all the wrongs that had been done against them; the past would be forgotten, and from that moment on, even their enemies would be considered as friends. The young woman gasped and said, "That's the word I've been searching for." Now it has been incorporated into their Bible. They are now able to read that when God places his arms around someone's shoulder, he is forgetting the past and even his former enemies become his friends.

I was not only interested, I was thrilled. There was good reason to be. Many years ago, my husband had been sent to New Guinea by the Australian Baptists. They wanted him to produce a film of what was being done by their missionaries. The people then lived in stone-age tribes. They still fought with bows and arrows, and, after a battle, often ate their prisoners. When the Lord comes into our throats, he will be able to inspire our testimonies and control our speech.

Blessed Are They Who Stand Tall

When we returned from one of our trips to Europe, we had many wonderful memories, but the most impressive concerns the city of Cologne and its magnificent cathedral. During World War II, the city was bombed 280 times, and on seven occasions the bombs hit the famous church. As you can imagine, the war left the city in a shambles. The great sanctuary, gaunt, desolate, and damaged, seemed to reflect the tragedy that had overwhelmed the world. But then, with holy resolution, the people of Cologne came forward to help in the restoration. They sold their pearls and precious jewels, and even then there must have been a surplus, for some of these priceless gifts can still be seen draped around the statue of the Madonna. The love of these folk overshone the gloom that had accompanied the destruction of their city. The citizens were standing tall amid the ruins.

The story is told of a man who lived in another city. It has been said that he made the mistake of placing a gold piece instead of a penny in the collection plate in church. Afterward, he went to an usher to ask for his gold coin. The usher objected, saying it would not look well if he took it back. "All right," said the giver, "after all, I have given it to God, and he will reward me for it." "Oh no, he won't," the usher contradicted, "God will reward you for only a penny, for that is all you intended to give." And in that moment of revelation, the giver was well and truly "cut down to his proper size." He wanted to stand tall in God's sight, but, actually, he was but a midget.

We saw many palaces and heard great stories of the exploits of certain princes, but nothing I heard equaled a story I had read years ago. It concerned a young prince with a crooked back. He was very sensitive about his deformity. Then one day, he commissioned a famous sculptor to make a statue of him. It had to be like him in every detail except for the back. The prince insisted that the spine be fine, tall, and straight. When the work was completed, the statue was placed in the palace gardens.

Thereafter, every day, the young prince stood, sometimes for hours, gazing at the work of art. What he was thinking about, no one knew, but after a while the palace guards began to ask, "Have you noticed the prince lately? His back is not as crooked as it used to be." Then, after several years they said, "Have you seen the prince? His back is as straight and as strong as ours." Looking up at the statue day after day, and month after month, the prince slowly had become what he wanted to be. I am reminded of the text that speaks about looking to Jesus (Heb. 12:2).

Whenever we gaze at ourselves, we become aware of the deformities that seem to beset us. We are not as tall as we would wish to be. We can only grow tall as we look to our Lord.

Blessed Are They Who Walk with God

"A nd Enoch walked with God: and he was not; for God took him" (Gen. 5:24). I once heard of a small child who was trying to describe the Enoch story. She said that Enoch went out one evening to take a walk with God. They went on and on together until they were closer to God's house than they were to Enoch's. So God said, "Why don't you come home with me?" And so Enoch did, and after he got there he liked it so much that he decided to stay.

Blessed are they who walk with the Lord, but it seems to me that sometimes the best way to walk with him is to stand still. Moses did this on the mountain and some of God's glory reflected on the face of his servant. Yet, in another sense, to walk with the Lord means daily progress. You cannot advance unless you move, keeping pace with him, matching him, as it were, step for step. Isaiah said, "But they that wait upon the LORD, shall renew their strength . . . they shall walk, and not faint" (Isa. 40:31). Alas, often we do not live according to this standard.

Outside one of the supermarkets where sometimes I shop, there is a mechanical horse. I have watched a mother put a dime into the coin slot, and to the joy of her child, the horse starts to gallop. When the time elapses, the horse suddenly gets tired and stops. The child and the horse are still in the same place where the adventure began. I see in this something which often happens to us. We get stimulated by some special meeting, which starts up our spiritual mechanism, our emotions are bounced around, but, after that exhilarating experience, we are not any further along than when we began. Walking implies continuance. If you have a particular destination in mind, you keep on walking until you get there. Enoch did just that—he walked all the way to his eternal home. What a man he must have been.

I read about a missionary who worked among the Eskimos. One man had good reason to dislike the white invaders of his territory. White trappers had stolen his seal skins and emptied his ice traps. Yet, he soon noticed that the "new" white people were different. They were kind and always tried to help others. These characteristics he had never before seen in such folk. They built a special igloo over which they placed a cross, and to this somewhat primitive sanctuary, they invited people to come to hear about a great Friend—Jesus. The man who had disliked white people so intensely attended services and one night stood up and said:

"I give to God a gallon of whale oil; I give him a fine sealskin; I now give God me, too."

Most of us are willing to give God of our possessions, but when it comes to the "me, too" we hesitate. We are prepared to walk just so far along the royal highway, but when something attractive is alongside the road, we lose sight of the eternal goal and cease walking. Surely, the secret of success is to keep our eyes on Jesus.

Blessed Is
the Love of a Mother

Recently, I found an article that appeared in our church magazine fifty years ago. I think you will find it interesting. These letters originally were given by Madeline Z. Doty in her book, *Short Rations,* and were quoted in *The Challenge,* December 6, 1918.

"It's your son," wrote the English airman. "I know you can't forgive me, for I killed him. But I want you to know he did not suffer; the end came quickly. He was very brave, and he must have been very good. He had your picture in his pocket. I am sending it back, though I would like to keep it. I suppose I am his enemy, though I don't feel so at all. I'd give my life to have him back. He was an enemy spy and I couldn't let him get back to tell his news. It meant death to our men. We were in brush, and he had to come low to see us. He was very brave. He nearly escaped me, for he handled his machine magnificently. I fired and it was over in a second. Just a blow on the head as his plane crashed. His face showed no suffering, only excitement. His eyes were bright and fearless. My mother died when I was a little boy. I know how she would have felt if I had been killed. I know his body must be dear to you. I will take care of it and mark his grave with a little cross. After the war, you may want to take him home. My heart is heavy. When I hold your picture in my hand, the war seems wrong. Oh, mother, be my mother just a little too, and tell me what to do."—Hugh

The German lady replied, "Dear Lad, There is nothing to forgive. I see you as you are—your troubled goodness. I feel you coming to me like a little child; astonished at having done ill, when you meant well. You seem my son. I am glad your hands cared for my other boy. I had rather you than any other touched his earthly body. He was my youngest. I think you saw his fineness. I know the torture of your heart since you have slain him. To women, brotherhood is a reality, for ALL men are our sons. That makes war a monster that brother must slay brother. Yet, perhaps women more than men are to blame for this world war. We did not think of the world's children as our children. The baby hands that clutched our breasts were so sweet, we forgot the hundred other baby hands stretched out to us. But earth does not forget—she mothers all. And now my heart aches with repentance. I long to take you in my arms and lay your head upon my breast, to make you feel kinship with all the earth. Help me, son, I need you. Spread the dream of oneness and love throughout all the world. When the war is over, come to me. I am waiting for you."—Deine Mutter

I think you will agree with me when I suggest that every person on earth should share the sentiments of these two people. Here is the challenge of the Bible, for the only thing capable of making the dream come true is the gospel. When, in the fullest and greatest sense, the love of God fills every heart, then war will be eternally outlawed. May that day soon come.

Blessed Are They Who Are Able to See Themselves

The other day, as I sat in the hairdressing salon, I became acutely aware of unusual activity all around me. Stylists were rushing all over the place; articles were being dusted, things placed in their proper position, and the entire salon made into a picture of neatness and loveliness. Then I heard someone say: "The inspector is coming." Another salon in Santa Barbara had phoned to give the warning, and the result was electrifying.

Later that day, as I looked through an old scrapbook in search of material for this chapter, I was thrilled to find the story of something that took place in our special meetings in Woodstock, Canada. The report said, "In Woodstock, a man recently dismissed from his employment because of excessive drunkenness, came into the meetings and ultimately accepted Christ as his Savior. The following Sunday, he brought his three children to church. They had never been inside any church in their lives. During the second week of the Crusade, his wife was also won for Christ, and I was thrilled to hear that their

158

first act in the new life was to clean their house from top to bottom. He who had spent his time and money on liquor, now knelt to pray and polish the floor. Later, as he stood beside his wife, he said, 'It's unbelievable—that this has happened to me. I never thought it was possible. It's unbelievable.'" I rejoiced again as I read the old report of the meetings in Canada, but the part that remained with me was, "Their first act in their new life was to clean their house from top to bottom." Probably, they had never really seen any dirt in their home until they had seen the Savior. When they saw him, they saw themselves—and their dirty surroundings.

Blessed indeed are they who are able to see themselves. The Word of God is the best mirror in the world. It not only reflects the beauty of the Lord Jesus, it helps us to see ourselves. The Lord said to his disciples, "Ye are clean through the word which I have spoken unto you" (John 15:3).

In our church in Wales, we had a young man who was so concerned about his personal appearance, his family said that it took him twenty minutes just to part his hair. He wanted to "look just right" when he met the young ladies in the meetings. He would peer long and hard into the mirror to see how he was progressing, and if he did not like what he saw, he ran the comb through his locks and started his grooming all over again. If only all of us would do that with the Word of God. If only we would spend time looking to see how we are progressing; how we look in the sight of God and man. If we did this, our appearance would be vastly improved and we would be far more attractive to those we live among day after day. Oh, to be like Jesus.

Blessed Are They Who Rest in the Lord

There is no way of knowing Mary's age when she gave birth to her son, but in all probability she was in her late teens or early twenties. In the East, marriage still takes place at an early age. Certainly, she was a remarkable woman. When told of the coming of the Savior, she replied, "Be it unto me according to thy word" (Luke 1:38). I have often heard my husband explaining that the penalty of illegitimacy in those days was death by stoning, and Mary was certainly aware of this. Her pregnancy meant she would be in terrible danger, yet, with perfect repose, she allowed her future to remain in the hands of God. Blessed are they who are able to rest in the Lord at all times. It is not easy, but it can be done.

Joseph Scriven was a fine Christian young man, eagerly contemplating his approaching marriage. But alas, on the eve of his wedding day his bride-to-be was accidentally drowned. What devastation. Yet, this young Christian remained calm, and as the years passed, he consecrated his life and fortune to the service of the Lord. He wrote the words, "What a Friend we have in Jesus, all our sins and griefs to bear. What a privilege to carry everything to God in prayer." I am sure that this was my father's favorite hymn. I often remember him as he sat rocking to and fro in his chair. His silky hair was snow-white; his face serene. He had been compelled to give up his beloved fishing, for his eyes were growing dim with age. So day after day he sat and rocked, and quietly sang, "What a Friend we have in Jesus." So many people question God and become disgruntled when He does not grant their every wish. When I think of my dad and Joseph Scriven and of that beautiful young mother, Mary, I pray that I might have their faith.

Throughout all the months of strain and wonder, Mary kept her balance. She was not overwhelmed by either worry or ecstasy, and I have been trying to discover the secrets of her triumph. What helped her reach those great heights of spiritual achievement? Obviously, she had yielded her life to God, and nothing was allowed to come between her soul and him. Also, she must have been very careful in her choice of a partner. The man with whom she intended to share the rest of her life was a good, godly, trustworthy man. Other younger men might have provided a different type of domesticity, but Joseph was not only her husband, he was God's man. And of course, she had a great friend in the hill country, Elizabeth, her aged cousin, who had an understanding soul. Oh, rest in the Lord.

Blessed Are They Who Climb Mountains

Yes, I have been thinking about the mountains for the last few weeks. Life is full of mountains and valleys. The air is always sweet and pure on the hilltop, but sometimes smog spoils the lower area. This is true in human experience also. Throughout the ages, people have enjoyed wonderful moments of ecstasy when they took time to scale the heights.

Sinai, Mount of Revelation. Two extremes of human actions are never more clearly seen than in the book of the Exodus. Down on the plains, Aaron and the children of Israel pleased themselves and made an idol. On the holy mountain, Moses talked with God until his face shone with the light of eternity (see Ex. 20).

Nebo, Mount of Repose. How strange and yet how wonderful it was that God was the only one to attend Moses' funeral. Perhaps even the angels stared in silence as God gently laid his servant to rest. Possibly, had the people known where to find the body, they would have made another shrine. The Lord knew what he was doing. But before Moses died, he was permitted to view the Promised Land. I think he had rest in his soul even before his body found it (see Deut. 34).

Transfiguration, Mount of Radiance. Thank God, death is *not* the end of the story. Although Moses died on Mount Nebo, we see him again speaking with the Lord on the Mount of Transfiguration. There, probably his entire being glowed with the glory of the infinite. Unlike Joshua and the people of Israel who had to fight their way into the land, Moses went in on the royal highway—he came down from the glory land. And since we are told he was speaking with Christ about the Cross (Luke 9:30–31), we can be sure that death had not ended Moses' ministry; it had deepened and enriched it.

Calvary, Mount of Redemption. This surely is the most wonderful hill in all the Bible. Throughout the centuries, millions of souls, by faith, have climbed it to exclaim in wonder, "My Lord and my God." I have seen the Himalayas in India, the Alps in Switzerland, and most of the great mountains of this world, but I was never so thrilled as I was on my twenty-fifth wedding anniversary when, with my husband, for the first time in my life, I actually climbed to the top of Mount Calvary.

The High Mountain, Mount of Rejoicing. "He carried me away . . . to a great and high mountain, and shewed me that great city, the holy Jerusalem, descending out of heaven from God" (Rev. 21:10). The last great revelation was given to John on a mountain. The job was finished, the victory won.

Yes, everything good seems to happen on a hilltop. Blessed indeed are they who climb the mountains, for they shall see God.

Blessed Are They Who Discover the Reason Why

The other day, I discovered an old Austrian folk tale that perfectly illustrates the meaning of Christmas. A village schoolmaster prided himself on being very intelligent and sensible. Before he would accept anything as a fact, he insisted on understanding logically why he should believe it. He claimed to be a good citizen but admitted that there was one thing about the Christmas story that he could not understand. Why should any God wish to take the form of a man?

Then, one snowy Christmas Eve, as he sat before his fireplace, he was feeling very smug about his rational attitude toward Christmas. Suddenly, he heard the noise of birds in the garden. This was strange, for it was a bitterly cold night. When the man looked through the window, he saw a flock of birds that had been forced down by the storm as they flew south. He felt sorry for the suffering creatures knowing that they must be very hungry. He threw out some crumbs, but alas, the birds were too cold and too frightened to eat. He reasoned that if he could lure them into the nearby barn, they might get warmer. He proceeded to lay a path of crumbs over the snow and all the way to the barn, but still they remained outside. Then he thought: *If only I were one of them they would not be afraid of me and I could lead them to safety.* It was at that moment that the church bells began to play Christmas carols and he had the reason why God became flesh and dwelt among us.

In an old issue of *Our Daily Bread,* the man who signs himself (H. G. B.) wrote the following story.

> An artist once drew a picture of a wintry twilight. The trees were heavily laden with snow, and a dreary, dark house stood bleakly in the midst of a storm. It was a sad picture. Then, with a quick stroke of a yellow crayon, the artist placed a light in one of the windows. The effect was magical. The entire scene was transformed into a vision of comfort and cheer. The Birth of Christ brought even greater illumination to this dark world.

You have all met people who do not believe the gospel. Have you ever visualized what the world would be like without Christ? There would be no Bibles, no churches, no Sunday schools. All the things that bring comfort, peace, and rest would be completely missing. The dying would have no solace, for there would be no news of life hereafter. The outlook would be completely bleak. But, thank God, his Son came to Bethlehem and lived in a stable. He knew the poverty of the human race, and because he stayed among us, he is now able to lead us to the warmth and shelter of the Father's "barn." I love all the holidays, but my favorite one is Christmas. It is so good to know he is still with us, and wonderful to know we can share our celebration with him.

Blessed Are the Lamplighters

One evening towards the end of his life, John Ruskin, the famous British author and art critic, sat at a window watching a lamplighter going on his evening rounds. With a torch in his hand, the man slowly climbed a distant hill, lighting one lamp after another. Since it was dark, the man could not be seen, but his progress up the hill could be observed as successive lamps were lit. After a few moments, Ruskin turned to a friend and said, "That illustrates what I mean by a genuine Christian. You may not know him, nor ever see him, but his way is marked by the lights he leaves burning."

When my husband was a very young preacher, he became associated with a band of traveling evangelists known throughout Britain as the Pilgrim Preachers. Their leader was Mr. Ernest Luff who owned a Bible store in Frinton-on-Sea, in Essex. He was a most wonderful man. His face radiated sunshine, and his long white beard reminded everyone of Santa Claus. One day on the street, a small child said to him, "Mister, are you Jesus?" He smiled and replied, "No, Honey, I am not Jesus, but I am trying to be like him."

This, to me, sums up the message of Christmas. The Savior came down into a very dark world to light a lamp that would never go out. From that initial light, others have lit their torches and have illuminated trails all over this world. How wonderful this is when compared with the trails of Communism. Their teachers leave behind evidence of discord, strife, and animosity. They breed discontent, wars, and murder. Yet, the messengers of peace take hope and happiness and even life itself to the people who sit in darkness and in the shadow of death. I cannot help but ask: "What kind of a trail have I left behind?"

I have also been thinking about the word *Christmas*. What does it really mean?

C is for comfort. The Christ of Christmas promises, "I will never leave thee, nor forsake thee" (Heb. 13:5).

H is for hope. "Christ in you, the hope of glory" (Col. 1:27).

R is for redemption. "In whom we have redemption through his blood" (Eph. 1:7).

I is for inspiration. "All scripture is given by inspiration of God" (2 Tim. 3:16).

S is for salvation. "Behold, now is the day of salvation" (2 Cor. 6:2).

T is for truth. "I am the way, the truth, and the life" (John 14:6).

M is for mercy. "The LORD is merciful and gracious . . . plenteous in mercy" (Ps. 103:8).

A is for assurance. "The work of righteousness shall be peace; and the effect of righteousness quietness and assurance for ever" (Isa. 32:17).

S is for satisfaction. "For he satisfieth the longing soul, and filleth the hungry soul with goodness" (Ps. 107:9).

Blessed Are They Who Obey the Traffic Signals

We live in a world where lights govern all of our living. The lights at traffic intersections tell us when to start and stop our cars. The lights on the microwave oven, the refrigerator, and washing machine signal various things. The tiny lights on the dashboard of the car warn us when oil is needed, when the car needs to be slowed down a bit, or when the radiator is about to boil over. As I look back over my life, I can even remember seeing lights beginning to flash in the eyes of angry people—the sure sign that a volcanic eruption was just around the corner. To ignore those silent warnings is harmful.

The Bible says that we are fearfully and wonderfully made, and I am sure all will agree with that statement. Our heavenly Father was so wise when he placed warning signals in our beings, and blessed indeed is the person who recognizes the tiny but significant flashes. Our bodies can only take so much. It is a mild form of suicide to go beyond those limits. I have had to learn this lesson all over again since my surgery. The doctors told me that as people get older, they naturally slow down; but when sickness comes, the slowing-down process is accelerated. They said I would have to live with it. Sometimes, in the middle of a very busy afternoon, I have been exhausted. The little light signaled, "stop and rest," but looking at the many jobs, I hesitated. However, I am slowly learning.

Our bodies and souls need rest periods. We can get uptight so very quickly, and this is not good. We become irritable, and then say and do things we do not really mean. Happy is the person who keeps an eye on the body's traffic lights. There is a time to stop—really stop. After a little while, we can start up again, and our brief pause along the highway of life reduces our chance of accidents.

Surely our Lord had this in mind when he invited the disciples to come apart and rest awhile. They had been so busy. Their nerves were uptight, and Jesus knew it. The body lights were saying, rest awhile; rest awhile.

Blessed Are the Sermons We See

Years ago, when my husband was the pastor of a church in Wales, we were fortunate in that God richly blessed the preaching of his word. From time to time, the Lord sent to us some of the choicest of his servants whose messages deepened our life of fellowship. Since that time, as you may know, we have traveled around the world and have been able to meet some of the greatest preachers on earth. Nevertheless, as I review those experiences, I admit that the greatest sermons ever to reach my life came not from the pulpit, but from the pew. A few days ago, I found a poem that expresses perfectly all I am trying to say:

SERMONS WE SEE

I'd rather *see* a sermon than hear one any day,
I'd rather one should walk with me than merely
    show the way.
The eye's a better pupil, and more willing than
    the ear;
Fine counsel is confusing, but example's always clear.
And the best of all the preachers are the men who
    live their creeds;

For to see the good in action is what every-
        body needs.
I can soon learn how to do it, if you'll let me see
        it done,
I can watch your hands in action, but your tongue
        too fast may run.
And the lectures you deliver may be very wise
        and true,
but I'd rather get my lesson by observing what
        you do;
For I may misunderstand you, and the high
        advice you give,
But there's no misunderstanding how you act and
        how you live.

> —Edgar A. Guest

Blessed are the sermons we see. I am sure you can think of people who fit into this picture. Some people are most eloquent with their lips, but they seem to stammer a little with their lives. Others, though too shy to speak, are most eloquent in their daily conduct. It has often been said that the only Bible some people read is found in human conduct. Years ago, the great evangelist, Gypsy Smith, used to sing a thrilling solo. The words were:

Can others see Jesus in me?
Can others see Jesus in me?
Oh, how shall the lost know of Jesus
If they cannot see Jesus in me?

Mr. Smith was a wonderful speaker, but many of his closest friends thought his message in song was even more effective than his sermons. Long ago there lived a man whose name was Enoch. It was said of him that he walked with God. He was also a prophet, but somehow, he does not seem to be remembered for his great speaking. His walk outshone his words.

Blessed Are They Who Never Quit

I have been looking at the photographs of seven young Russians who are now in prison. Their story makes me feel very small. The Bible is full of accounts that tell of unflinching courage. Daniel walked bravely into the lion's den, and young David challenged the giant, Goliath. The entire world is aware of the exploits of the patriarchs, but today, I wonder if the men of old could equal the courage of some of our brethren in other lands.

In the August 1975 edition of *Freedom*, the magazine of Russia for Christ, along with a photograph of the seven men is the following message:

> There are several printing presses in the U.S.S.R., run by Christians and condemned by the government. These presses print Bibles, hymnbooks, copies of *Pilgrim's Progress*, and news sheets presenting case histories of imprisoned Christians.
>
> The seven young believers for several years ran one of these presses in a forest near Ligatne,

Latvia, producing thousands of pieces of Christian literature. On October 28, 1974, while these seven men were kneeling by their press and surrounded by 30,000 New Testaments, either completely printed or in process of being produced, from one to two hundred secret service policemen (members of the K.G.B.) surrounded the building where the press was located and arrested the Christian printers. Within days, another such press was printing the photographs of these seven believers along with a detailed account of the K.G.B.'s break-in. Missionary societies in many nations are focusing world attention on this case, using for the defense of the captured Christians, one of the weapons most feared by the Communists—FACTS.

What would we do if we lived in Russia? If I dwelt there, I, too, would be in prison for writing this book. For many of our brothers and sisters in other lands, *it costs* to be a Christian, *but they never quit*. For us, it is so easy. Alas, many people complain about the slightest difficulty, and every excuse is used to avoid the responsibility of doing one's utmost for Christ. We sometimes give so little to him who gave his all. Let us place our hands once more on the plow and get on with our task.

Blessed Are God's Pencils

During a visit to the Baptist camp in the Tehatchape Mountains, I found a copy of *McCall's Magazine*, and as I read an article about Mother Teresa, my heart was strangely warmed. This wonderful missionary to India grew up as a grocer's daughter in a small town in Yugoslavia, but she became an international symbol of goodness. Yet, she wanted no credit, insisting that God was only using her to write a love letter to the world. In the slums of Calcutta, they called her a saint. In the leprosy camps of Bengal and Madras, she was an angel in a white sari who worked miracles. In the corridors of India's government, she was a woman to be respected. In Ceylon, Venezuela, Tanzania, and the Bronx, she was a mother whose church had no walls because it extended to wherever a crippled person crawled, a child lay abandoned, or an old person waited alone and forgotten. She was Mother Teresa of Calcutta, a tiny woman who emerged from cloistered walls to work in the slums of India. In the end she was awarded the Nobel Prize for peace. *McCall's* said,

> No single person in the entire Catholic Church
> of 500 million, popes included, has been honored
> as this five foot nun who was born of Albanian

parents in Skoplje, Yugoslavia, and christened Agnes Conxha Bojaxhiu. While other orders struggle with loss of members and recruitment, Mother Teresa's initial band of 12 has expanded into a worldwide order of more than 1800 nuns, 275 brothers, and 120,000 lay co-workers who minister to the sick, the dying, and the destitute in 31 countries. In Calcutta alone, there are 3,000 slums. It has become known as the "nightmare city." She said, "No one thinks of the pen while writing a letter. Readers only wish to know the mind of the person who wrote the letter. That's exactly what I am in God's hand—a little pencil. God is writing a love letter to the world in this way, through works of love."

A little pencil. Not even an ornate, much-prized fountain pen. No, just a little pencil in God's hand. As I read the account of the amazing exploits of this woman, I began to understand why God must be so proud of his servant. The warmth of her love has radiated throughout continents, and surely millions will call her blessed.

We are not all called to go overseas as missionaries; we are not all expected to take a leading part in church, but surely we can all become little pencils firmly grasped in the Master's hand. God wishes to express his mind through us in a simple, marvelous way so many souls will find it easy to understand how wonderful the love of our heavenly Father is. What are we writing today? When people read our message, will they frown or smile? Will they be lifted in spirit to heaven, or plunged deeper into the depths of unhappiness and despair? Some of the modern pencils or pens often run dry; others are scratchy and annoying; some run smoothly, responding to every suggestion coming from the Writer's hand. I hope I am usable. I would like to write something wonderful today.

Blessed Are God's Superstars

O ne night at a party in honor of my husband's birthday, I met a remarkable young man. He was only one week old in the Christian faith, but already the light of his faith in Christ was shining in his eyes. Just over a week before, he had been a paid political agitator; an avowed Communist agent whose mission in life was to destroy all faith in the Christian religion. At a special Communist rally in Los Angeles, he was blasting away on his portable loudspeaker, attracting a crowd, when an insignificant old lady with piercing eyes quietly slipped a gospel tract into the pocket of this outrageous young fellow who was denouncing her God. Without saying a word, she deposited her tract and then, just as quietly, walked away.

That unknown woman would surely have the shock of her life if she knew that the speaker at that meeting is now a fine, growing, glowing Christian. By day and by night her piercing eyes haunted that Communist, and finally, remembering she had placed something in the pocket of his jacket, he lifted out the pamphlet, read its message, and became a very frightened man. He fled from Los Angeles and his Communist friends and in Santa Barbara met a Christian who led him to Christ. He attended Bible classes for three or four hours every day, and it is truly amazing how much of the Bible he learned in just over seven days. There is no way of telling now what he might become, but one thing is obvious—he will owe everything to the grace of God and the little old lady with the piercing eyes. She has already attained greatness in the sight of God. She is one of his superstars.

A long, long time ago, there was another woman like her. She, too, was a superstar, but only the Lord recognized that fact. All that she did was done quietly and without fuss, but the ever watchful eye of Jesus saw and spoke of the inestimable worth of her deed.

> And Jesus sat over against the treasury, and beheld how the people cast money into the treasury: and many that were rich cast in much. And there came a certain poor widow, and she threw in two mites, which make a farthing. And he called unto him his disciples, and saith unto them . . . this poor widow hath cast more in, than all they which have cast into the treasury: For all they did cast in of their abundance; but she of her want did cast in all that she had, even all her living (Mark 12:41–44).

Sometimes games are won, not by the fellow who hits the baseball out of the park, but by the quiet little player who makes all the defensive moves to prevent the other team from scoring. God knows his players. Blessed indeed are his superstars.

Blessed Are the Eyes That Can See

Some time ago, as I listened to a television hostess, I became keenly interested when she said: "Don't grumble because roses have thorns, just be thankful that thorns have roses." This statement made a profound impression on my mind. Dr. Norman Vincent Peale has written a book about the importance of thinking positively in all circumstances of life. It is not always easy to do this, and it often hurts when we try.

Sometimes it is much easier and much more compelling to look on the negative side of things, but this breeds doubt, fear, and sorrow. I think Paul might have appreciated the statement about the thorns having roses, for during his lifetime, he knew what it meant to have a thorn in the flesh. Many preachers have wondered what that thorn might have been. Perhaps God planned that we should not know. Paul's text can apply to all kinds of our own situations. With John Wesley, the thorn was a nagging, unsympathetic wife who even disrupted his meetings. With many people, the thorn is a troublesome physical ailment. Some pastors have more than one thorn in the flesh—they have six or seven on the deacons' board. Certain parents have thorny teenagers, and I have known a few wives who were continually hurt by the attitude and actions of husbands who thought they were never wrong about anything. Oh yes, I am quite sure that every reader will have firsthand experience with thorns in the flesh. How easy it would be, on occasion, to permit these nasty things to color our entire outlook, to become highly sensitive or irritable, always ready to hit out at those near us.

Many of life's great people reached that exalted position because of their wonderful ability to see roses among thorns. John Bunyan, the saint imprisoned in Bedford, England, refused to spend his time grumbling about his circumstances— instead, he wrote *Pilgrim's Progress*. The great Creator ordained that even baby chicks have to struggle to break through a shell to gain entry to the big world. To help the tiny thing would almost destroy it. This struggle develops the chick's muscles and prepares it for life in a waiting world. The same God knows all about us. Happy indeed are we who see and know that, in spite of the thorns, the beauty of the blossoming rose more than compensates for any pain we experience in possessing it.

Blessed Are They Who Thrive in the Desert

The other morning, as I was reading the sixth chapter of Mark, I was impressed by one simple statement. Mark referred to the "desert place" to which the people went as they followed Jesus. I knew, of course, that this meant an "uninhabited place; a place that had never been cultivated." Oftentimes during our tours of Israel, we have journeyed through these inhospitable areas and have marveled at the rocks strewn over the landscape. Mark tells us in verse 39 that, in spite of this being a desert area, the people sat on green grass.

His simple but dynamic statement transported me to the land of Israel. If there were green grass, there must have been water in the vicinity. A well or an oasis must have been nearby and, from this source, came moisture to nourish the velvety cushion on which the people sat.

As I read the words, it seemed to me that the very setting of Mark's story provided a parable. Life is filled with desert places, and the outlook sometimes can be extremely bleak and barren. Nevertheless, the very presence of Christ guarantees that living water is at hand. Did he not say: "If any man thirst, let him come unto me, and drink" (John 7:37).

Our home in Wales was called "Elim," which means "the place of refreshment" (see Exod. 15:27). We chose this name because it expressed the longing of our souls. It was our desire that many people, wandering in the stony wilderness of life, would enter our door and find comfort. Yes, it was our constant prayer that tired people would find "green grass" in our home. And, thank God, this happened on many, many occasions.

Perhaps the most amazing experience of green grass is described for us in Genesis. Jacob, having deceived his father and robbed his brother of the cherished birthright, fled to a place called Haran, which was very far out in the desert. The day was far spent and the sun was setting when this weary man gathered stones to be used as a pillow. He not only slept in the desert, he had lived in one all his life. He had been an artful scoundrel, skilled in the doubtful art of using his wits. Yet, that night he discovered that God was also in the desert, and before dawn arrived, he saw a ladder that ascended into the very presence of the Lord. Years later, when basically still a crook, he wrestled with an angel in the night and finally he had green grass on which his soul could repose. Even our desert places can become watered gardens if we recognize that God is there. I think I would much prefer to be in a desert with God than in a well-watered garden without him. Wouldn't you?

> Son of my soul, Thou Savior dear
> It is not night if Thou art near;
> Oh, may no earth-born cloud arise
> To hide Thee from Thy servant's eyes.

Blessed indeed are they who find green grass in the desert.

Blessed Are the Plans of God

Someone said: "The man who removed the mountain, started by carrying away small stones." This statement provides food for thought. Perhaps one of our greatest weaknesses is *impatience*—we want to accomplish so much, but we want things done immediately. If we fail, we fret, and sometimes this shows in our conduct and attitude. A small stone at a time does not seem much, but a small stone removed every day soon becomes a truckload. Are you facing mountainous problems—physical, domestic, financial? Why not seek encouragement in the above philosophy, and begin removing your problems one at a time, a day at a time, yes, even a prayer at a time. Often, it is far better to exercise your faith by lifting a stone than it is to grow despondent watching the approaching shadow of a great mountain. Always remember, the Lord has a plan for your life, and he is still working at it. The writer, George McDonald, describes a man who grumbled, "I don't know why God ever made me." His friend replied, "But God has not made you—yet. He is still making you, and you do not like what he is doing." At the moment we are God's unfinished business, but we may be very sure he always completes what he commences.

John Augustus Roebling, who designed the Brooklyn Bridge, was confined to his bed during the period of construction. When the bridge was completed, the great architect was placed in a small boat, propped up with pillows, and taken to a strategic viewing point in the East River. The blueprints were in his hands as he viewed the awesome construction. After a long silence, in which his eyes scanned every part of the steel giant, Roebling, with a smile of pride upon his face, leaned back and said, "It's just like the plan. It's just like the plan."

Paul says God planned that we be conformed to the image of his Son. Thank God, when the work is finished, the Great Builder will proudly survey his handiwork and say, "They are just as I planned."

Blessed Are the Swivel-chair Christians

The other day, I was reading a Charlie Brown cartoon, and I was fascinated by the way in which the creator of these characters, Charles Schultz, had captured one of the greatest lessons in life. Lucy, the philosopher-like girl in the series had told Charlie that life was like a deck chair. She explained to her puzzled friend that passengers on a cruise ship open up their chairs so that they can sit in the sun. She said that some of them sit in the rear of the ship so that they can see where they have been. Others, face their chairs forward so that they can see where they are going. Then, with the directness of an evangelist, she drove home her point by asking, "On the cruise ship of life, Charlie Brown, which way is your deck chair facing?" Poor Charlie was nonplussed and replied, "I don't know. I have never been able to open the thing."

All who have traveled on ships can understand Charlie's problem. Some of us are forever looking back; others, despising the past, are always looking forward and hoping. Blessed are they who can look both ways and profit by doing so.

The psalmist in Psalm 105:5 urges his readers to remember the marvelous works that God has done. Moses, in one of his greatest speeches, said to Israel, "And remember that thou wast a servant in the land of Egypt, and that the LORD thy God brought thee out thence through a mighty hand and by a stretched out arm" (Deut. 5:15). It is both wise and beneficial to look back and remember all the favors and blessings sent by God. We must forget not all his benefits. Even when we get to heaven, we may still look back and say with Fanny Crosby:

> All the way my Savior leads me
> Oh, the fullness of his love
> Perfect rest to me is promised
> In my Father's house above.
> When my spirit clothed immortal,
> Wings its flight to realms of day;
> This my song through endless ages,
> Jesus led me all the way.

To look back is to be reassured, for never once has the Lord failed us. Yet, we must not be content with just looking back— we are going somewhere. Happy and blessed is the swivel-chair Christian, who, remembering this, will turn to survey the journey ahead. I am sure that Paul did not possess a chair of this type when he sat alone in the prison in Rome, but within his radiant soul he certainly had the capacity to look both backward and forward. In 2 Timothy 4:7–8, he was certainly looking back when he said, "I have fought a good fight, I have finished my course, I have kept the faith." He was surely looking ahead when he continued, "Henceforth there is laid up for me a crown of righteousness, which the Lord, the righteous judge, shall give at that day: and not to me only, but unto all them also that love his appearing." When you have read my words, look back over your life and remember his grace, then, with hope and trust look on through the day and sing.

Blessed Are They Who Rise Above Their Circumstances

During our stay in Spanish Wells, in the Bahama Islands, I found an interesting poem that I want to share with you.

Old Jim had been a faithful horse
But he was growing old;
So Uncle Lem made up his mind
The horse should not be sold.
But turned out in the pasture land
To roam and feed at will
Or rest beneath the shady trees
Down by the waters still.
Lem loved his faithful servant, Jim,
And watched him day by day
And when he whistled to the horse
Jim gave an answering neigh.
One day the horse had disappeared
So Lem went out to see
What had become of faithful Jim

Where could the creature be?
Lem thought of an abandoned well
Which had uncovered been.
He hurried down the path to see,
Yes, Jim had fallen in.
If he should try to pull him out
A leg might broken be;
So he would go and get his gun,
And end Jim's misery.
Lem brought the gun but couldn't bear
To shoot old faithful Jim;
So brought a shovel and a pick
With which to bury him.
Lem took a shovel full of dirt
And rolled it in the well,
It slid down on the horse's back
And to the bottom fell.
As fast as every load was sent
The horse would stamp it down
And as they both thus worked away
At last the well was gone.
Out jumped the horse, all whole and sound
Kicked up his heels and ran.
Let's get from out this simple tale
A moral, if we can.
When people try to crush us down
And cover us with dirt;
Let's stamp it underneath our feet
And never let it hurt.
Let's be like Jim and rise above
The troubles that beset,
If we are on the side of right
We'll gain the victory yet!

—Author Unknown

Perhaps one of the most difficult verses in the Bible to believe is found in Romans 8:28: "And we know that all things work together for good to them that love God, to them who are the called according to his purpose." *All* things do not mean *some* things. Only real faith can grasp such promises. It is very hard to appreciate falling dirt when enemy hands are holding the shovel. Yet, if God is truly in charge of every operation touching our lives, all is well.

Blessed Are They Who Know How to Give

During one of our journeys, my husband and I stopped at one of the Big Boy family restaurants. Later, when we went to the cash desk to pay for our meal, the young cashier gave us an informative card about the early pioneers who helped lay the foundations of this great country. With increasing and very real interest I read about Nathan Hale. He only lived for twenty-one years, but he left behind a legacy which will live forever.

He was born on June 5, 1755, in Coventry, Connecticut, graduated from Yale College at the age of eighteen, and thereafter taught school in New London, Connecticut. He lived in those troubled times when the early pioneers were torn between two affections. The old loyalty to England sometimes seemed incompatible with the deep-rooted desire for freedom from tyranny. The imposition of fresh taxation and New England's resistance inevitably led to conflict. Hale joined the army as a lieutenant in 1775 and was promoted to the rank of captain the following year.

When new soldiers arrived from England, the situation assumed threatening dimensions, and General Washington became worried about the ever-increasing strength of the foe. It was imperative that someone penetrate the enemy lines in search of information. In September 1976, Washington called for volunteers to undertake this suicidal mission. His men listened but remained silent. Then one man stepped forward. That man was Nathan Hale. He was completely untrained in espionage, but his commander needed a man, and he was determined to be the one.

Slowly, but surely, he passed through the enemy lines, and ultimately succeeded in gaining information about the British fortifications in New York. Posing as a schoolmaster, he wrote his notes in Latin and hid them in the sole of his shoe. He crossed Long Island and began his journey back to General Washington's headquarters in Manhattan. Alas, he was captured by the British who found the hidden papers. When Nathan Hale bravely admitted his role with the American Army, he was, without trial, condemned to death by hanging on September 22, 1776. His last words were: "I only regret that I have but one life to give for my country." He gave all that he had, and neither man nor country could ask for more. Out of the travail of those dread years, came this wonderful land—the United States of America.

We have a cause; we have a Leader, God's own General who came down from heaven. If he should ask for some special service, will we step forward to exclaim: "Here am I"? Blessed are the givers.

Blessed Are the Dirty Knees

At one time I read the story of a young Scotsman about to leave his homeland. Just prior to his departure, he decided to go for one last walk in the heather out on the hills. He knew he might never have a chance to do this again. He was not only facing a new year, he was facing a fresh start in a strange country. As he walked, he came upon an old shepherd herding his sheep in a quiet glen. As they talked, the shepherd whistled to his sheepdog, and with great skill, the animal ran around in narrowing circles until the sheep were in a compact group. As usual, the lambs were surrounded by the rest of the flock. The shepherd reached in with his crook, hooked a lamb around the neck with its curved end, and eased the youngster out. He did this with each lamb and then returned them to their place, all except two.

He passed one to the Scotsman along with an infant's bottle and asked him to feed it. He fed the other one himself.

The young man asked, "How did you know which lambs were not being fed?"

The shepherd replied, "Their knees were not dirty." The lambs had not been down on their knees taking nourishment from their mother.

I was greatly impressed by this story, for if our souls are to be nourished, we must be "on our knees" looking to God for food. Perhaps this is the most important thing I can say as we face the future. Doubtless, we shall all experience difficulties and problems, and there may come days when we shall not fully understand nor appreciate the working of God on our behalf. Nevertheless, if we really pray and trust, we shall know that even the strangest dealings of the Lord have an unfailing purpose.

While a small boy watched, his precious sailing boat drifted further and further out on the surface of a great pond. Desperate, he asked a bigger boy to help him. He could not understand why the older lad began to throw stones at the drifting toy. It did not seem as if he were helping. Then he detected that each stone was falling *behind* the small boat. As a result, each new ripple caused by the falling stones was bringing back the lost treasure. Behind each stone was a carefully thought-out plan. The older boy knew what he was doing. This is the message I wish to send to you. Some events in your future may seem to suggest that God is throwing stones *at* you. Remember the hand that throws the stone is called love. It belongs to your heavenly Father.

Blessed Are They Who Know Where to Find Shelter

O ver thirty years ago, Mr. Harold J. Shepstone, a fellow of the Royal Geographical Society of Britain, wrote a remarkable article concerning the air-raid protection for the ancient city of Jerusalem. He said, "No city anywhere possesses such a unique, and so far as that goes, historic air-raid shelter as Jerusalem. It is a very serviceable one. Indeed, the Holy City's warden declares it to be 100 percent bomb-proof; safer, in fact, than London's underground railway." This shelter is nothing less than a vast cavern beneath the city; it is known as Solomon's quarries, from the belief it was here that Solomon obtained the stone for the building of the temple. Its story is quite a romantic one.

The quarry was accidentally discovered in 1852 by an Englishman named Barclay. He was out with his dog when the animal suddenly dashed off in pursuit of some bird or animal. The dog disappeared behind some bushes near the old walls close to the Damascus gate and then began to bark as if in distress. Hastening to the spot, Barclay found that the dog had fallen down a crevice. The animal was quickly rescued, but on examining the crevice, Barclay discovered that it led under the wall and the city to a vast cavern that extended a distance of several hundred feet. After a careful examination, it was found to be a vast quarry. It ran in a straight line in a southerly direction for just over one thousand feet, and spread out to a considerable width in some places. The roof was supported by great pillars of rock. Here, no doubt, the workmen had labored and prepared the stones for Solomon's temple. Engineers now declare that there has been sufficient stone taken from these quarries to build Old Jerusalem three times.

The Bible tells us that the stones for the temple were prepared in a quarry and that "there was neither hammer nor ax, nor any tool of iron heard in the house, while it was in building" (1 Kings 6:7). The noise in this great underground chamber would not be heard in the temple area though it was not far away.

Opinions vary as to how many people could be accommodated in the quarries. The wardens state that at least ten thousand people could be housed with very little preparation. Anyone sheltering there would know he had at least twenty to fifty feet of solid rock above his head before the streets of Jerusalem were reached. Thus, the world's greatest and most extensive underground quarries founded by King Solomon over three thousand years ago, can be used to protect the inhabitants of Jerusalem from any air attack. How wonderful it is to know, too, that every new discovery on ancient sites only adds to the overwhelming mass of evidence proving the Bible is true.

I shall always remember when I first walked through those historic quarries. I knew I was treading where ancient workmen had toiled for their king. The floor was very slippery, and progress was slow. It was easy to forget the present and to go back in thought to the times when these caverns rang with the shouts of overseers and workmen; when history was being made. I thought of another hiding place not far away— a little hill called Calvary. The Bible tells of the cities of refuge in ancient Israel, and describes how the gates were never closed by day or night. At any time, a person needing to find shelter was able to do so. I knew when I stood on the green hill that this was the greatest hiding place of all time.

Life has taught us all that there are many different kinds of air raids in which Christians are blitzed and battered by Satan's "war planes." Sometimes, out of a clear blue sky, and without warning, evil missiles fall to shatter our peace and threaten our future. Pity, indeed, the poor soul who has no shelter.

> Beneath the cross of Jesus
> I fain would take my stand,
> The shadow of a mighty rock
> Within a weary land.
> A home within the wilderness,
> A rest upon the way.
> From the burning of the noontide heat—
> And the burden of the day.
> O safe and happy shelter
> O refuge tried and sweet.

Blessed are they who know where to find shelter; but even more blessed are the people who go there often.

Blessed Are the Peanuts

I have always had a liking for peanuts, but since President Carter was elected to high office, in common with millions of other people, I have become increasingly interested in his kind of nut. The other day, I found in my collection of old newspaper cuttings, a most interesting article. It is said that George Washington Carver, the famous black American researcher, once asked, "Lord, what is the universe?"

The Lord replied, "George, that's too big for your little head. Suppose you let me take care of the universe."

Greatly humbled, the scientist asked, "Then Lord, if the universe is too big for me to understand, please tell me what is a peanut."

And then the Lord answered, "Now George, you've got something your own size. A peanut can understand a peanut; go to work on the peanut while I run the universe."

George Washington Carver went to work on this project at the Tuskegee Institute in Alabama. He revolutionized southern agriculture by finding a use for the peanut. Instead of depleting the soil by repeated crops of cotton, the farmers grew peanuts to enrich the ground of the plantations. These peanuts became big business and today are the main crop in many areas. Among many other items, Carver took peanuts and made cheese, milk, butter, flour, ink, dyes, soap, stains, and insulating board.

The more I read, the more amazed I became. This great man, George Washington Carver, was born in 1864 of slave parents near Diamond Cove, Missouri. Before he was two months old, he and his mother were kidnapped by night riders and carried into Arkansas. His mother was never found, but Carver was ransomed by his original owner for a horse valued at $300. When about ten years old, he left the farm where he had been born and eventually settled in Minneapolis. There, he worked his way through high school. In 1894, he graduated from Iowa State College of Agriculture and Mechanic Arts. He joined the college faculty, specializing in bacteriological laboratory work in systematic botany. In 1896, he became director of the Department of Agricultural Research at Tuskegee Institute where he began his tremendous experiments with peanuts. He also did extensive research with the sweet potato, eventually producing shoe blacking, library paste, vinegar, starch, candy, and more than 110 other useful substances from it. He developed a new type of cotton known as Carver's Hybrid, and he manufactured synthetic marble from wood shavings, and dyes from tomato vines, beans, dandelions, onions, trees, and clay. For all this work, he was honored internationally and, in 1940, he donated his life savings to the establishment of the Carver Foundation for Research in Creative Chemistry. His birthplace became a National Monument in 1951 (from *Funk and Wagnall's Encyclopedia*).

I think you will appreciate my feelings. When I had finished reading the achievements of this remarkable man, I was left somewhat breathless. Obviously, the Lord was able to see all that was in a peanut, but when he told George a peanut could understand a peanut, he also knew what was in the head of that human peanut. The breadth of his life is unbelievable. Kidnapped and held for ransom at two months of age, bought back for the price of a horse, this unknown, ignorant slave boy reached unprecedented heights of international glory. I am beginning to wonder if I have ever done anything worthwhile. When I gave this beatitude to my husband, he read it and said, "Boy, I look at a peanut and see a cause for indigestion. That fellow looked at it and saw a goldmine." I think that about sums it up.

Doubtless, the Lord was able to see the end from the beginning. He who sees a strong oak tree in every acorn saw in the peanut inestimable treasure. Carver was told to work with the peanut while God ran the universe, and he did not argue. He succeeded beyond his wildest dreams. Surely, little is much when God is in it.

The other day, a friend of ours was describing what had been left after a certain woman died. She said, "She only left peanuts." Actually, the amount was $500. But to her, that amount was so pitiably small that it was nothing. It is marvelous what God can do with peanuts. Sometimes we may feel as insignificant, as small, and as useless as a nut. When that happens, remember, God made the peanut, and he knew what he was doing.

Blessed Are They Who Listen

As long as I live I shall remember our visit to Alaska. I saw many strange and wonderful sights, but my greatest memory will always be our trip through Glacier Bay to the Muir Glacier. The official handbook supplies the following information.

> When Captain George Vancouver sailed through the ice-choked waters of Icy Straight in 1794, Glacier Bay was little more than a dent in the shoreline. Across the head of this apparently minor inlet stood a towering wall of ice—a wall that marked the seaward outlet of an immense glacier that completely filled the broad, deep basin of what is now Glacier Bay. To the north, ice extended more than 100 miles covering the basin to widths of 20 miles. In many places, the ice was 4,000 feet thick. Today, the ice has receded almost 80 miles. Muir Glacier receded five miles in just seven years. As water undermines the ice-fronts, great blocks of ice—up to 200 feet high, break loose and crash into the sea, creating huge waves and filling the narrow inlets

with massive icebergs. The glaciers discharge
such great volumes of ice that it is seldom possible to get closer to their cliffs than 2 miles.

We were most fortunate that during the time of our visit,
the water was comparatively free of icebergs and, as a result,
our ship was able to sail to within a few hundred yards of
those gigantic ice cliffs. Suddenly, we were looking at a solid
face of jagged ice two hundred feet high, and a mile and a half
wide. Unlike the ice we make in our refrigerators, this ice was
a beautiful blue-white and begged description. It was
majestic, awesome, and yet, in other remote ways, almost
terrifying. The handbook told us that during a severe earthquake in 1958, an estimated eighty-two million metric tons of
rock, weakened by glacial erosion, broke loose from the cliffs
above the terminus of Lituya Glacier. Thundering down the
mountain, the slide tore one thousand feet of ice from the
terminus and crashed it into the water. On the ridge opposite
the slide, a wave surged to a height of 1,720 feet, then moved
seaward completely stripping four square miles of forest from
the shores. Evidence of this giant wave's destructive power
will be visible for years.

The rangers who came aboard our vessel explained the ter-
minology used in connection with the formation of the icebergs. When a great lump of ice breaks free from the glacier, it
is referred to as "calving." The parent glacier has given birth
to a calf. We were all intrigued when over the public address
system of the ship, a ranger said, "I am going to stop talking
so you can hear the glacier speaking to you." We listened in
the silence. It was easy to hear the continual groaning and
ripping as the relentless river of ice slowly moving forward,
literally tearing rocks, dirt, and even trees from the mountains. Sometimes when the ice cracked, the sounds resembled
rifle shots. The loud speakers crackled again, and a voice said,
"Listen, can you hear the glacier speaking?"

Just at that point, the ranger lost my attention. Earlier, in the ship's cinema, my husband had concluded the interdenominational religious service by saying, "Now, as we go on deck to see the wonders of God's handiwork, let us remember we have already talked with the One who made all we shall be seeing." Suddenly, I was seeing the glacier of life. I was hearing all the groanings and moanings as the pressures of life seem to tear at our souls. And then it was so easy to listen to another voice which said: "Be still and know that I am God. . . . There shall no evil befall thee, neither shall any plague come nigh they dwelling. For he shall give his angels charge over thee, to keep thee in all thy ways" (see Pss. 46 and 91). Then my soul seemed to sing, "How great thou art, how great thou art." Yes, my heavenly Father held all those glaciers in the hollow of his hand. He made all of the majestic hills and the sky above them. He made it all, and yet, somehow, though he was and still is so great, he loves me and holds me safely in the hollow of his hand. Have you felt lately that the pressures of life have been too great, that everything of value had been torn from you? Has life's glacier been tearing at your peace of mind? Just listen.

Blessed Are They Who Have the Right Bondsman

It was Sunday night, it was late, and most of the prisoners in the Santa Barbara jail were quiet. My friend, Brother Charles, the chaplain of the local prison system, was slowly making his way toward a certain cell when a raucous voice yelled, "Hey, Preacher."

The chaplain paused, and then turned to see a man peering through the bars of his cell door.

"You are the preacher, aren't you?" the convict asked. "We want out of here; we want a bondsman."

Brother Charles, beloved by so many of the Santa Barbara citizens, said, "We?"

The man replied, "Yes, my brother and I want out. Can you arrange it for us?"

The chaplain slowly looked at the stranger and answered, "Well, yes, I suppose I can, but what kind of a bondsman do you want?"

"What d'ya mean," replied the prisoner. "I don't care what kind, but we want to get out of here fast."

"Well," continued the chaplain, "There is the usual bondsman and he will charge you between three and four hundred dollars. What he will do is only temporary, because eventually you will have to appear before the judge, and if you are guilty, you will end up back in this cell. Now there is another one, and he does his work without a fee. You don't have to pay him, and if he gets you free, you will be free indeed. He can get the Judge to pardon you."

"Hey man. That's the one we want. Get him for us fast. What's his name?"

By this time the silence of the prison had been shattered. Other convicts were at their cell doors listening. The prisoners were truly excited. Brother Charles surely seemed to tantalize them when he paused to say, "Well, there are certain conditions attached before this bondsman will take your case. You have to plead guilty. As soon as you do this, he can get on with the task of getting you out of prison." Then Brother Charles told them about the Lord Jesus—the greatest Bondsman the world has ever known—the one who comes to us when we are penniless, hopeless, and friendless. He told them about the Lord Jesus who is actually the Son of the greatest Judge of all. He explained how the Savior ever lives to make intercession for us, and because of his tremendous love for sinners, he is both able and willing to be our helper at any time of the day or night. And then the miracle happened. The same blessed Holy Spirit who moved upon the face of the deep at the beginning of time, moved upon the depths of two sinful hearts, and the light of the gospel shone into the darkness.

As amazement spread over their faces, two prisoners suddenly threw their arms around each other and danced on the floor of their cell. Actually, they were brothers from northern California, but within seconds, they were brothers in the Lord. As the chaplain told his story, his eyes had grown misty, yet still they shone with the light that can only come from God. It is wonderful to watch the birth of a spiritual baby.

That is the message I want to bring to you. Have you ever wished on the first of January that you could see ahead to the things that would happen before the end of the year? Sometimes I have, but I am not sure that this would be good for us. The Lord surely wants us to live one day at a time, to meet the challenges of each new day as it comes.

> I cannot read His future plans,
> But this I know;
> I have the smiling of His face,
> And all the refuge of His grace
> While here below.
> Enough. This covers all my wants
> And so I rest.
> For what I cannot, He can see,
> And in His care, I safe shall be
> Forever blest.

We need never be lonely; we are not alone. We have a Bondsman. It is not that we are outrageous criminals spending our time in prison; it is not that we are among the vilest on earth—though sometimes we may think we are. It is rather that we are so prone to get into trouble. Something goes wrong, we worry, we get irritable, and then before we know where we are, we are truly in bondage. It is so nice to remember that our Savior understands. He knows all that there is to know about us, and he loves us just the same. He can and he will get us out of prison fast. If you forget all else that I have ever written, please remember this message. We have a Bondsman. We really do.

Blessed Are They Who Love the Quietness

There is a text in God's Word that says, "Be still (quiet) and know that I am God." Have you ever been surrounded by so much noise and confusion that you felt like pulling out your hair? Peace and serenity seemed a million miles away while you were surrounded by noise, noise, noise. A little while ago, I was in this unfortunate position, and there was not much I could do about it. Piped music from a nearby swimming pool played all day long, and a guest in the next room watched his TV from 5:00 P.M. until 2:00 A.M. Our annoying neighbor usually went to sleep—and then we did—about two-thirty, but at five in the morning, loud, thunderous banging announced to everybody that it was time for the construction worker next door to arise and go to work. Oh, how wonderful it was when we moved away to another area and *felt* the quietness.

It is so necessary, whenever possible, to get away from all the commotion of this world, just to rest and sit down with God. He said, "In quietness and in confidence shall be your strength" (Isa. 30:15). Even our Lord knew the value of this, for he invited his disciples to come apart and rest awhile. The old hymn says: "Take time to be holy, speak oft with thy Lord."

How long is it since we made time to sit in a garden and listen to the song of a bird or made the time to listen to a small child lisping out a story? How long since we knelt in a quiet, hallowed spot to listen to the still small voice of the Holy Spirit? Perhaps if we pause to seek answers to these questions, a searchlight will shine into the depths of our souls to reveal spiritual qualities. If we are too busy to do this, then we are too busy.

Even David became aware of this need in his life, for a small bird revealed to him the necessity of building a home in the quietness. The psalmist said, "Yea, the sparrow hath found an house . . . even thine altars, O LORD of hosts" (Ps. 84:3). Out in the world was danger, but close to the altar of God was peace and safety. The little bird knew it, David knew it, and thank God, we can know it also.

Perhaps today you are so keyed up with the noise and tension of daily living; the ever-recurring meals; the yelling of the children, the grumbling of some members of the family; the telephone, television, and radio; the barking of dogs—noise, noise, noise—you feel like adding to it by screaming.

The hymnist said, "There is a calm, a sure retreat, 'tis found beneath the mercy seat." Do you remember how it is written that Moses stayed forty days alone with God in the mountain, and though he was unaware of the change, his face shone? It is impossible to linger in the presence of God without being changed. Somehow, some of the glory of God rubs off on us. We need to be quiet, to be still, and thus see the hand and face of God.

Blessed Is
the Cactus Plant

A while ago, I proudly carried into our covered patio a flower pot containing a gorgeous cactus plant. On it were two beautiful flower buds. I was really excited as I looked forward to seeing the buds blooming, but the next morning they seemed to have shriveled and died—yet, they were not dead. This puzzled me until I realized the cactus belonged to the night-blooming variety. Fascinated by all this, I read in *Funk and Wagnall's Encyclopedia* the following details:

> Most cacti are leafless, prickly and grotesquely formed as a result of environmental adaptation. The stems are green, fleshy and succulent; well adapted for storing water throughout long periods of drought, and usually globular or cylindrical in shape. The leaflessness of cacti reduces evaporation to a minimum, and the spiny surface serves as a protection against thirsty, herbivorous desert animals. Long spreading roots draw up all available moisture, which is retained in the plant for long periods of time. The best known representative of the tribe Cerei is the night blooming cereus.

The author did not tell me why this particular variety blooms in the dark when other plants would find this impossible. As I thought about the matter, the Bible began to suggest that the cactus plant might have its counterpart in some very special Christians. After all is said and done, any flower can bloom in the sunshine; it demands something special to do so in the dark. Our roots must spread out to gather whatever moisture is available from God. We must learn how to store it and refrain from wasting our precious supply. We must recognize also the presence of enemies who would deplete our resources and weaken our resistance. So we learn how to repel their attacks. In fact, as with the cactus plant, we recognize we are living in a desertlike world that ultimately only leads to death, and this very realization makes us work all the harder at driving our roots toward the living water. The night-blooming cactus is a very special plant. No ordinary eye will see it, but it is there; wonderful, attractive, a beautiful thing shining like another kind of star on a very dark night. When fog and dampness fill the air, the scent of the unseen flowers drifts along on the night breezes, and in some remarkable fashion, the atmosphere becomes fresh and wonderfully alive.

Job was a night-flowering plant. In the midst of his troubles he said, "Though he slay me, yet will I trust him." I heard only yesterday of an Indian leper who gave her testimony in the hospital where she was being treated. When she lifted her hand, it was without fingers or thumb. She said, "I would rather be a leper and have Christ, than to have a healthy body and not have Christ." Even as she said it, a perfume came out of her night of suffering— a perfume seldom known among folk upon whom the sunlight falls. Perhaps H. G. Spafford had this in mind when he wrote:

When peace like a river attendeth my way
When sorrows like sea billows roll,
Whatever my lot, thou hast taught me to say,
It is well, it is well with my soul.

Blessed indeed is the Christian whose beauty shines in the night. That soul is very precious in the sight of God.

Blessed Is the God of Silver Linings

We have lived in Santa Barbara, California, for many years, and during that time have experienced numerous earthquake shocks. Yet, the quake that shook our city some years ago was different. Many of the inhabitants were scared by falling glassware and other household items, and we were all left to wonder what might have happened had that shock lasted longer. For a little while, it seemed like invisible hands had gripped our home and were shaking it as a dog would shake a bone. Seashells came tumbling down from the shelves in my husband's shell room; crystal vases and ornaments fell from walls and cupboards. We resembled Olympic athletes as we speedily left our home for the comparative safety of open spaces. During the next thirty or more minutes, the earth continued to tremble beneath our feet, but soon calm was restored. The quake had subsided.

As the days passed, we began to see evidence of silver linings. For example, a freight train had been derailed north of the city. The track had spread-eagled and the locomotive and carriages had plowed into the earth. Behind it was a passenger train with four hundred people. The derailment had brought all other traffic to a standstill and, thus, the passenger train did not overturn as the freight train had.

Probably the most thrilling story is the one that did not make the headlines in the newspapers.

We have in our city a remarkable man known as Brother Charles who is the official, though unpaid, chaplain of our prisons. At the moment the earthquake rocked our district, Brother Charles was counseling a convict. When the walls began to sway, the prisoner yelled, "Brother Charles—pray—pray. I'm not ready to die."

The next day he was visiting in a nearby city, but alas, his clients were not at home. After knocking at the door repeatedly, he went to the next house to ask if the occupants had any idea where Mr. and Mrs.— might be. The neighbor did not know, but when Brother Charles explained that he had come all the way from Santa Barbara to see these people, the man exclaimed, "Santa Barbara. My, you had an earthquake up there."

"Yes," responded Charles, "I was in prison at the time."

"In *prison?*"

"Yes, in prison, I was speaking with a prisoner in a very small cell. And when that building rocked, the convict said, 'Pray, pray, Brother Charles. I am not ready. I am not ready.'"

The listening man said, "He was not ready? Ready for what?"

Charles replied, "He was not ready to die, of course," and then grasping his opportunity, added, "Sir, would you be ready to die?"

The man replied, "Oh, I am a Baptist."

The chaplain continued, "Sir, I did not ask that . . . I asked if you would be ready to die?"

Quietly, the man said, "No."

There on the lawn in front of the house Brother Charles explained the gospel message, and at last the neighbor was really saved. As joy and peace flooded his soul, he said, "This is my spiritual birthday."

It had taken the full force of an earthquake to shake him from his complacency as a very inactive Baptist. The neighbor explained how he had been baptized as a child, but it had very little meaning for him. Just as they were finishing their conversation, Brother Charles's clients came home from the supermarket where they had been shopping, and once again silver linings could be seen in the clouds. Had they been at home earlier, the man next door would have remained a very contented, very complacent, but very unprepared church member—not ready to die. I cannot help but wonder if God had this in mind even before he permitted the quake to scare the life out of the citizens of our fair city.

Isn't it good to know that our heavenly Father can make all things work together for us if only we have the sense to trust him. So many of our treasures come tumbling from the walls of our lives during the weeks and months and years. And then we ask: Why? Sometimes it is hard to answer that question. As I have so often said, "God works in a mysterious way, His wonders to perform. He plants his footsteps in the sea, and He rides upon the storm." But, even in earthquakes, he is never very far away, and his hand is always steady. Rest in it.

Blessed Are
the Redwood Christians

A people great . . . and tall." (Deut. 2:10). I thought of this text as I stood in a forest of giant redwood trees. My eyes became a little moist as I looked at those magnificent specimens of God's creative power. The beautiful trees were straight and tall as they reached toward the sky; their foliage and branches seemed like giant heads spread out in adoration and thanks to almighty God. Oh, how my soul yearned that I, too, would appear straight and tall before him.

Later, in the family camp, I heard Lt. Col. Dechert of the United States Army give his testimony. This fine Christian man had been a member of the famed Green Berets and had been assigned to a most important position in Vietnam. Among his varying other duties, he was in charge of security and was responsible for the safety of 150 children in a Christian and Missionary Alliance school. He told us that at that time he was only a nominal Christian, but as such, he had attended a very special prayer meeting that had changed his life.

Three missionaries had been kidnapped by the Communists and were in very grave danger. There was little their colleagues could do except pray, and this they did. In a very simple hall they knelt on the rough cement floor and stayed there for hours. They were so intent on interceding for the captives that they seemed unaware of their own suffering. The colonel said that when the missionary ladies eventually rose to their feet, their *knees were bleeding*. Of course, they had prayed for the captured missionaries, but paramount in their intercession was the request that somehow their colleagues would be able to win their captors for Christ.

Those marvelous Alliance missionaries were a people great and tall, but they were never quite as tall as when they knelt on that cement floor. Mrs. Mitchell, the wife of one of those captives, waited hopefully as the years passed. Her soul was thrilled when the news was announced that all prisoners in Vietnamese hands would be coming home, but alas, when the lists were read, Mr. Mitchell's name was missing. Representation was made in the highest political circles to ascertain the whereabouts of the missing captives, but finally the news came that Mr. Mitchell and his coworkers had died in captivity. This was truly devastating to all who had waited so long. Yet, that delightful woman, Mrs. Mitchell, would not accept the news. She fully expects her husband, one day, to come walking out of those jungles.

Lt. Col. Dechert described the many hours shared in prayer with those missionaries, but as I listened to him, I asked myself how my prayer life compared with what I had heard. Oh, to be as the redwood trees. Some days, down at ground level, the fog is swirling and visibility is poor, yet up aloft, the tops of those marvelous trees are bathed in sunshine. I shall never forget them. Blessed indeed, are those people who stand great and tall.

Blessed Are They Who Have Found the Hiding Place

There are many wonderful verses in the book of Isaiah, but perhaps one of the best is found in chapter 32:2. "And a man shall be as an hiding place from the wind, and a covert [shelter] from the tempest." Even when I was a child, I knew the value of a good hiding place, for when our family was visited by friends, the children often played hide and seek. Those games that I played so long ago seem to have added significance now.

Probably the prophet had often witnessed the tremendous power of a storm, when the howling winds turned placid waters into a raging tempest and when the unrestrained power of wind whipped the sand like particles of steel into the unprotected faces of travelers. Any hiding place is a welcome refuge in a storm. With children, hiding is a game; with adults it becomes a glorious refuge. Blessed indeed are they who have found the Hiding Place.

Isaiah said, "A man shall be as an hiding place from the wind," and that same prophet spoke eloquently of the coming Messiah. He surely saw and understood what Christ would become to his people. There are many and varied storms that try the patience and endurance of God's people, but in them all the Savior can become our hiding place. Some of our best hymns were inspired by this truth. John Wesley, the great preacher-poet, was walking one day in the country when a small bird, chased by a hawk, flew beneath his coat to seek safety. The bird had found a hiding place. Wesley thereupon wrote, "Jesus, lover of my soul, let me to thy bosom fly."

A. M. Toplady, another British hymnist, was walking in the lanes of Somersetshire when he was suddenly caught in a terrible storm. Noticing a deep cleft in the rocky hillside along the roadway, Toplady climbed into the deep crevice and stayed there until the storm had passed. A strange and perhaps mystical warmth flooded his soul, and he wrote, "Rock of Ages, cleft for me, let me hide myself in thee." He too knew of the great Hiding Place.

Readers will understand what I mean when I confess that it is easy to become disturbed, to worry, to become frantic about things. Isaiah also said, "Their strength is to sit still" (30:7). Is it possible that some of you might be needing this message? Is a storm beating down on your soul? Don't worry. Find the Hiding Place—and sit still.

Blessed Are They Who Watch

Recently, I was loaned a book about prophecy. It was called *Time of the End*, but when I examined its contents, I was surprised to discover the volume was 117 years old. It was published in 1857, and contained excerpts from sermons preached by many of the old divines, including John Wesley and Martin Luther.

As I read the words of these great men, I was charmed by the message of Horatius Bonar. Expressing the beliefs of the church, he said, "My kingdom is at hand; my sun is about to rise. I shall soon see the King in his beauty; I shall soon be keeping festival, and the joy of my promised morning will make me forget that I ever wept."

Beyond the difficulties of this life, the church can see New Salem, the city of righteousness. Bonar emphasized that for the church, this is the night watch (Mark 13:35–37). It is the prospect of morning and of the Master's return that keeps it watching. This is especially true when we realize that watch after watch has come and gone, and he has not yet arrived (Hos. 6:3). It is to watching that the church is specially called.

The church is called to believe, but that is not all—it has also to watch. The church will be known throughout the ages as the watching one.

The world may ask, "Why stand ye gazing up into heaven?" Our reply must be, "I am watching."

People may ask, "Why not have a good time, why not live things up?" (1 Peter 4:4). The church replies, "I am watching."

Even Satan might suggest, "Why not have a vacation and rest from your spiritual exercise?" The church replies, "I dare not, my Lord said: Watch." This is the secret of its spiritual strength and vitality. When other institutions ask, "How are you so strong?" The church answers, "I watch." "How can you resist temptation?" "I watch." "How can you love, forgive, and check fretfulness and anxiety? How can you be strong when others are weak? How can you be patient when others are restless and grumbling? How can you be satisfied with little, when others continually demand more of this world's goods? How can you wrestle with grief and banish tears when other people sink into despair?" The church replies: "I am watching."

Faith alone is insufficient; even love is not enough. Faith focuses the soul on its desired object, and love keeps the vision in focus. But expectation and obedience must go hand in hand with faith and love along the path of life, and while the going may often be rough and the road steep and winding, the eyes of the soul are ever upward—we watch for the dawning of the day. At all times our lamps must be trimmed. Why? Because we do not know at what hour our Lord might come.

Yes, blessed indeed are they who know how to watch. I am reminded of the disappointment that the Lord knew when he found his disciples asleep in the Garden of Gethsemane. Throughout this time of sorrow and anguish, when his blood mingled with his tears, his disciples had slept. He sighed, surely, as he asked, "Could ye not watch with me one hour?" And then with compassion that outshone all else, Jesus added, "The spirit indeed is willing, but the flesh is weak." If only Peter or John had held his hand—but they were no longer watching; they were asleep. What an opportunity was lost that night. Amidst the crises of life we must watch and keep on watching.

Blessed Are They Who Know the Meaning of Christmas

I have just been reading in a very old book that the legends linked with the genial figure of Santa Claus probably originated in the generous deeds of Saint Nicholas, a bishop of Myra in Greece during the fourth century. This wealthy man delighted in helping poor families secretly, until, at last, his identity was discovered. Since then, all anonymous gifts have been attributed to the kindly saint. Saint Nicholas Day is actually celebrated on the sixth of December, and in Belgium small children eagerly look forward to the coming of Santa Claus, who is supposed to ride over the house tops. He is said to come on a white horse or donkey carrying a basket filled with toys and candy. On the eve of this great day, the children place an offering of hay and carrots near to the chimney so that the horse will not be hungry. When they awake in the morning, they hurry to see if the offering has been taken. This is the sign that they have been good. If they have been naughty and disobedient, they are disappointed to see a birch rod stuck in the hay. It is said that such practices in one form or another may be found all around the world. To the young, this is the

meaning of Christmas. To many older folk, Christmas is a time
for feasting and merrymaking. But to all wise people, Christmas means much, much more. We praise God because the
angels over Bethlehem's fields gave us an example. We enjoy
good food because the best of all food—the Bread of Life—
came to us at Christmas. We give gifts to each other because
that is what God did when he gave us his beloved Son. We
worship at the feet of the Savior; we adore him because ever
since the Magi did this two thousand years ago, the greatest
of earth's people have followed their example. It is nice to be
in good company. Christmas without Christ would be a farce.
Love that never reaches out to some other person is only a
mirage—something without substance. These are the thoughts
that fill my mind as I approach this great time of the year. As
we meet together in family gatherings, let us say a special
prayer of thanksgiving. In all our rejoicing let us remember
the goodness of God.

> What can I give Him, poor as I am?
> If I were a shepherd, I would bring a lamb;
> If I were a wise man, I would do my part;
> Yet, what can I give Him:
> Give Him my heart.

Blessed Are
the Chickenhearted

Whoever invented the word *chickenhearted* didn't know his chicken. *Chickenhearted,* according to Webster's Dictionary means "to be timid, afraid, fearful, or cowardly." In our modern language, anyone without courage is said to be "chicken." We have become accustomed to hearing from anyone backing off from a dangerous task: "I chickened out." I was interested recently to read the words of the late Dr. M. R. De Haan who wrote:

> Chickens are not cowardly. Take the case of my hen. I had placed fourteen eggs under her, and she faithfully hatched all fourteen. That took courage and stamina and patience for twenty-one long days. I made a coop for her with slats across the open end, so that the chicks could pass in and out while the mother remained inside. That coop was outside my study window. One afternoon a storm arose, but before it broke, I could hear the frantic "cluck, cluck" of the mother hen as she called her brood to shelter. It was a terrible storm. Trees were blown down and the air was filled with debris.

Suddenly a gust of wind blew the coop into the air and sent it tumbling across the lawn. I was expecting hen and chicks to be blown all over the place. But there she sat on the open lawn without shelter, exposed to a gale violent enough to blow a man down. As though she were cemented to the ground, she squatted motionless until the storm had ended. Don't ask me how she did it. I think love for her little chicks had made her immovable. Now we can understand why Jesus compared His own love to that of a hen who "doth gather her brood under her wings" (Luke 13:34).

Not too long ago, my husband and I were conducting an evangelistic crusade in an area where sick men seemed to find pleasure in cock-fighting. They reinforced the claws of the birds with talons of steel, and while the onlookers yelled approval, the birds, rather than quit, literally fought until one died.

No, chickens are anything but cowardly. The person who coined the word *chickenhearted* did not know his chicken. On the other hand, the Lord certainly did, and it is interesting to note how he included them in his preaching. For example, in the text already mentioned he seems to remind us of his love. Later, in connection with Peter's denial, it was the crowing of the cock that brought Peter to his knees in true repentance. Perhaps there the Lord was suggesting we should listen more carefully to what he says to us. But maybe the greatest text of all is in Mark 13:35 where the time of the cockcrowing is linked to the return of the Master. Surely this teaches us the absolute necessity of always being on the lookout. The next time you see a chicken, remember my words. As God has loved us, so we must love and listen to him. And as we love and listen to him, we must always look for him.